Praise for 7 Ways to Powers

I found it to be very enlightening, inspirational, full of insights and common sense advice regarding our daily spiritual living... I would highly recommend it in trying to find a balance on your path in the progress of your own spiritual development with God.

-Maddie Wingett

V.M. GOPAUL helps the reader understand the inner spiritual meaning of concepts and terms encountered in the scriptures of religion, such as being 'born again,' and the 'rapture' predicted to occur at the end of the world when the dead will be raised from their graves.

-Carla Jeffords

All characters appearing in this work are fictitious. Any resemblance to real persons, living or dead, is purely coincidental.

7 WAYS TO OBTAIN DIVINE GIFTS AND POWERS

All rights reserved.

Copyright © 2014 V. M. GOPAUL

No part of this publication may be reproduced, stored in a retrieval system, or transmitted, in any form, or by any means, electronic, mechanical, photocopying, recording, or otherwise, without the prior consent of the author vmgopaul@gmail.com

Visit our website at www.vmgopaul.com

This book is available for purchase, in print and e-book formats, through FastPencil, Amazon and Barnes & Nobles

Cover Design by Melissa J. Moores

Original background photograph: *Clouds & Sun Rays* by Jim Pennucci - flickr April 26, 2011

7 WAYS TO OBTAIN DIVINE GIFTS AND POWERS

V. M. GOPAUL

All rights reserved.
Copyright © 2014 V. M. GOPAUL

UNITYWORKS
NEWMARKET, ON

Table of Contents

TO THE READER	IV
INTRODUCTION	VI
CHAPTER 1 - SPIRITUAL BIRTH	1
CHAPTER 2 - KNOWLEDGE OF GOD	13
CHAPTER 3 - LOVE OF GOD	33
CHAPTER 4 - SPIRIT OF FAITH	49
CHAPTER 5 - PHILANTHROPIC DEEDS	65
CHAPTER 6 - SELF-SACRIFICE	81
CHAPTER 7 - SEVERANCE FROM THIS WORLD	99
CHAPTER 8 - SANCTITY	113
APPENDIX A	127
BIBLIOGRAPHY	129
REFERENCE	131
ACKNOWLEDGEMENT	137
ABOUT THE AUTHOR	139

To the reader

When researching and writing this book, I directed my attention to the scriptures of world religions, such as Judaism, Hinduism, Buddhism, Christianity, Islam and the Bahá'í Faith. To me, they are authentic source of spiritual guidance and wisdom.

In our material world, explaining and understanding spiritual concepts can present us with many challenges. Therefore, I also turned to nature. In many ways it mirrors the worlds beyond.

Finally, I studied human experience in the application of divine concepts and how spiritual living has benefitted mankind.

When reading this book you will notice many references to the writings of Bahá'u'lláh, the founder of the Bahá'í Faith. As you will see later, the idea of "7 Ways to Obtain Divine Gifts and Powers" came from 'Abdu'l-Bahá, the son of the Prophet. In Appendix A, you will find a list of websites where authoritative, comprehensive information can be found about the Bahá'í Faith, in case you are not familiar with it.

Introduction

One occupation common to all humans is the search for happiness. Over the ages many paths have been tried. Some climb the highest mountain to find the elixir of life; some are consumed in their profession; still others are engaged totally in ascetic life of yoga, meditation, and charity. In the Bahá'í Faith, the key to happiness is a balanced life. A traveler will never be satisfied with just one goal. Humans are multi-faceted and complex beings. This means education, career, family life, and charity are all important, but all must be seen through a spiritual eye. In my estimation, positive action, executed with a clear, divine vision will bring the soul the greatest possible satisfaction.

Cultivating a Healthy Spiritual Lifestyle

We care a lot about our bodies. Breathing, eating, and drinking are routine activities that maintain our health by supplying vitamins, proteins, minerals and other essentials to our bodies. We spend a significant amount of time daily to earn money, go grocery shopping and cook meals. If we get sick we receive medical care from doctors, nurses, pharmacists, and dietitians. Individuals, families, governments, and industry work together for our common physical benefit.

    We cannot say the same for our spiritual wellbeing. If a soul is concerned about its health, most of the time it's on its own, without help from the government. Of course, there are religious groups as well as other associations that provide help to those in need of spiritual or psychological assistance. However, the Bahá'í Faith aims to unite all hearts in one universal Cause, one common Faith, and invites all of humanity, no matter what race or religion, to participate in such a civilization-building process.

    To promote this universal goal, let's look at some activities individuals and groups can partake in to maintain a thriving community, where spirit and body are given equal importance. As Bahá'ís, we believe that we exist in an organic relationship with our environment. Individuals and societies are inseparable; in fact, each influences the other. Some of the teachings and activities of the Bahá'í Faith are:

- Daily obligatory prayer
- The Nineteen Day Feast, during which the members of the community read devotions, consult about matters of the Faith in their community, and socialize
- An annual fast, lasting nineteen days
- Study circles, a sequence of courses on spirituality, designed to develop qualities, attitudes, and capacities necessary for service to humanity
- Thoughtful, daily reading of the Bahá'í Writings
- Engaging in work or a profession is considered as worship to God if it is done in the spirit of service
- The pursuit of education and the teaching of others are so highly regarded that they are considered the same as participating in services at a church, mosque, temple, or synagogue
- Pilgrimage is recommended as a way to connect to the lives of the Central Figures of the Bahá'í Faith
- Regional and national Bahá'í Schools are organized throughout the year, where believers go for weekends or whole weeks to study Bahá'í Writings as a way to replenish the soul and discover ways to apply the spiritual teachings in their lives.

- Local children's classes
- Devotional meetings
- Recitation of the Greatest Name (Alláh-u-Abhá, meaning God is the most glorious) ninety-five times daily
- Living life according to Bahá'í principles

These are just a few examples of how to provide your soul with the food it needs. Just as we make serious efforts to maintain a healthy physical being, our soul does not grow on its own. We must strive to develop our spiritual qualities.

What happens when a soul does not make a conscientious effort to improve its wellbeing? Though one may experience a second birth or enlightenment, the spirit can also die without proper sustenance. The consequences of spiritual negligence are subtle. You don't see it coming, until one day you realize something is wrong. Should you realize what went wrong, you will wish you could turn back the clock.

When the body is not functioning there are immediate signs: usually some sort of pain. Fortunately; there are signals of inner malaise as well. But we have to learn how to listen for them, as they are not always as obvious as physical signals. Here are some of them:

- Emptiness. You may not have any physical, emotional, or material problems, yet you think life should be more than just daily existence.
- Negligence. Negligence can be characterized as not participating in activities that replenish the soul.
- Ego. If you are too occupied with yourself rather than others, you may find that life is not really satisfying. Many studies have demonstrated that those with higher goals, like serving others, are happier than those who are self-centered. A person may have many outward successes, but inside they can still be searching for a clear direction.
- Fault finding. 'Abdu'l-Bahá told a group, "Let your thoughts dwell on your own spiritual development, and close your eyes to the deficiencies of other souls." [1]
- Apathy, or an absence of interest in spiritual development.
- Imbalance. A balanced adult life consists of work, family, recreation, and faith. Sometimes we end up spending too much time on one of these and end up

neglecting the others. Demands at work may leave little time for other important activities. This can create conflicts internally and externally. Once in a while it is good to pause and examine all your activities, reflect on them and see if recalibration is needed.

- Prejudices. They are veils separating us from the truth. Bahá'u'lláh exhorts us to strive daily to eliminate all prejudice
- Disobedience. Disregard for laws may come from our lower nature. Gaining an understanding of why laws are essential in maintaining order in our lives, in society, and in the whole universe can make us appreciate the true freedom obedience brings. Just like the physical laws that govern the universe, social and spiritual laws not only guarantee us a peaceful existence, but are the building blocks humans need to prosper.

Many of these obstacles are caused by our lower nature, so one way to overcome them is to shift our focus to a higher level of consciousness. An elevated purpose can be achieved through acquiring virtues and perfections, according to 'Abdu'l-Bahá. He explains:

By what means can man acquire these things? How shall he obtain these merciful gifts and powers? First, through the knowledge of God. Second, through the love of God. Third, through faith. Fourth, through philanthropic deeds. Fifth, through self-sacrifice. Sixth, through severance from this world. Seventh, through sanctity and holiness.[2]

In the coming chapters, we'll examine these seven topics in more detail. Before we proceed, let us be mindful of one important warning. Too often, plans don't unfold as expected. In our spiritual journey to paradise there will certainly be hurdles, delays, and derailments. But there are three things that one can do to reach the finish line safely.

Preparedness: Just imagine yourself climbing Mount Everest. Would you stuff some clothes in a bag and, with sandals on your feet, start your ascent? You will have to build your stamina for such an arduous climb. Oxygen becomes scarce as you scale the heights of the mountain; therefore, a good supply is a must. Food, proper clothing, and a durable tent are a just few of the things a mountaineer would need to pack before taking the first step, and sufficient time must be allowed to prepare, reach the mountain in the right season, and make the climb. A spiritual traveler must also be well prepared. Here are more things that can be in your spiritual "cabinet"

Accountability: Bahá'u'lláh teaches us to "Bring thyself to account each day ere thou art summoned to a reckoning..."[3] A wise climber will, before resting for the night, reflect on how well the day went. Did they cover the distance they planned to cover? Are they physically able to continue traveling? How are their companions doing? For mountaineers, climbing the highest peak is their dream, and they would do everything in their power to make it come true. Conquering Mount Everest will be their happiest moment. The same resolve is needed on our spiritual path.

Assistance: A spiritual journey is always full of surprises, difficulties, and confusion. You will not reach the highest point in this journey by relying entirely on yourself. No one is truly successful without God's help. The essence of spirituality is the soul's realization of all its weakness when facing the Almighty. When this awareness has dawned upon the traveler, they begin to draw strength from the ocean of Divine powers.

7 Ways to Obtain Divine Gifts and Powers   xv

CHAPTER 1

Spiritual Birth

The Gopaul family, with the help and encouragement of Mandana, decided to host a regular devotional gathering in order to unite with others in prayer and shape a pattern of life distinguished by its devotional character. We wanted this gathering to be special by combining prayers with short conversations on related spiritual subjects. Every heart longs to commune with its Maker. Reading the Holy Verses uplifts our spirit and brings us closer to God. From these ideas, we hope participation, sharing and learning will naturally occur.

Each devotional and deeper learning would focus on a particular theme. The themes build on each other in order to advance our understanding of spiritual topics, based on 'Abdu'l-Bahá's statement previously mentioned.

Devotion

☼

O Thou Whose face is the object of my adoration, Whose beauty is my sanctuary, Whose habitation is my goal, Whose praise is my hope, Whose providence is my companion, Whose love is the cause of my being, Whose mention is my solace, Whose nearness is my desire, Whose presence is my dearest wish and highest aspiration, I entreat Thee not to withhold from me the things Thou didst ordain for the chosen ones among Thy servants. Supply me, then, with the good of this world and of the next.

Thou, truly, art the King of all men. There is no God but Thee, the Ever-Forgiving, the Most Generous.[1]

☼

My God, my Adored One, my King, my Desire! What tongue can voice my thanks to Thee? I was heedless, Thou didst awaken me. I had turned back from Thee, Thou didst graciously aid me to turn towards Thee. I was as one dead, Thou didst quicken me with the water of life. I was withered, Thou didst revive me with the heavenly stream of Thine utterance which hath flowed forth from the Pen of the All-Merciful.

O Divine Providence! All existence is begotten by Thy bounty; deprive it not of the waters of Thy generosity, neither do Thou withhold it from the ocean of Thy mercy. I beseech Thee to aid and assist me at all times and under all conditions, and seek from the heaven of Thy grace Thine ancient favor. Thou art, in truth, the Lord of bounty, and the Sovereign of the kingdom of eternity.[2]

☼

Deeper Learning

One thing is certain: every human being arrives in this world in a naked and fragile body. After this physical birth, a newborn is in desperate need of others for survival. Fortunately, there is always help nearby for the new arrival, who holds promises of developing physically, emotionally and intellectually, of being educated, reaching self-sufficiency and becoming a productive citizen of society. Then, after a life here, death surely comes, sometimes unexpectedly. This is the life of a human being on this planet in a nutshell.

There is another kind of birth. Of all the religions, Christianity particularly emphasizes this second birth. In fact, there are even "Born Again" Christians. This has to do with what Jesus Christ said. According to John, Jesus said: "Except a man be born again, he cannot see the Kingdom of God."[3] Jesus also said, "That which is born of the flesh is flesh; and that which is born of the Spirit is spirit"[4]. These sayings suggest that there are two realities to a human being: the physical and the spiritual. Through our physical birth we enter this world, but to gain access to the Kingdom of God, we need to experience a spiritual birth.

According to 'Abdu'l-Bahá, the Kingdom of God refers to a world beyond the physical. He said:

> Therefore, in this world he must prepare himself for the life beyond. That which he needs in the world of the Kingdom must be obtained here.[5]

These quotations suggest that we need to experience transformation to condition ourselves for the next world, just as in the womb we are transformed from a single cell to an infant in preparation for this world.

To be spiritually born involves gaining awareness that our existence is not only physical. Those who profess to have experienced this spiritual dimension understand that their existence is highly enhanced when they live according to spiritual laws and not only by the dictates of physical and social impulses. The highest point of this awareness is to acknowledge that there is a supreme divine Being, called God or Allah or Yaheveh, Who is the creator of the universe. When one who goes through this rebirth, that person also understands that the soul, our inner spirit, must develop a relationship with this Supreme Power for its own good.

What to do with this knowledge? For those who take it seriously, life could be a wonderful experience. With it one can ride the waves of difficulties that life throws at us. It gives meaning to existence beyond the physical realm. When we die, life does not end; rather it continues throughout eternity. Without this understanding, life is only the here and now. Have a good time. Look after me, me, and me.

Finding God is a personal journey, and our experiences along the way are as unique as we are. For example, my friend in Alberta, Canada, was looking out at a majestic landscape when suddenly she realized that a Supreme Power must have created all that she saw. This was her moment of awakening. She investigated many religions and eventually became a Bahá'í. My own experience was different. At the age of fifteen, I concluded that God did not exist. A few years later, I came across the Bahá'í Faith. The Bahá'ís eagerly informed me of their beliefs and gently pressed me to become a member, but, at the time I had very little appetite for religion. In 1969, I went from my birthplace of Mauritius to Pakistan to study. In Karachi I contacted the Bahá'ís, who were friendly and hospitable. Nine months later when I decided to leave Pakistan and head towards Europe by road, one Bahá'í suggested that I contract the Bahá'ís on my journey. It sounded like a good idea and I immediately accepted. During my travels in Europe, I was always in touch with the Bahá'ís and participated in activities whenever possible. In 1971, I reached Toronto and realized that I was very much part of this religion, yet I still did not believe in God.

Knowing that religion is fundamentally about a relationship between the soul and God, I felt hypocritical in calling myself a Bahá'í. Immediately after this realization, I started my quest for God. After a few months of reflection, I came to the same conclusion as I had when I was fifteen: there is no God. I was disheartened and wondered what I did wrong. Then the answer came. I was using my mind to logically satisfy myself of the existence of a spiritual Being. It wasn't until later, at a meeting where prayers were being said, that my approach changed. I began to use my heart to sense the presence of the Almighty. With faith, I had to make the first move and, sure enough a spiritual awareness came to me.

These two stories show that divine assistance is easier to call upon than dialing 911. In the Qur'án, it is said, "And whoso maketh efforts for Us, in Our ways will We guide them: for God is assuredly with those who do righteous deeds."[5]

During this second birth, something even more profound than the initial awakening takes place: the Holy Spirit, a signal telling the soul of a higher existence, touches your soul. This is the moment when a real spiritual life starts. With this direct interaction between a willing soul and the Holy Spirit, its recreation begins. It is a new journey to see and reflect the Beauty of God.

To the early believers, Bahá'u'lláh said: "...ye are the first among men to be re-created by His Spirit, the first to adore and bow the knee before Him, the first to circle round His throne of glory. I swear by Him Who hath caused Me to reveal whatever hath pleased Him! Ye are better known to the inmates of the Kingdom on high than ye are known to your own selves."[7]

Briefly, let's go through some of the differences between the physical and spiritual birth. The physical birth just happens. No one asks for your permission. Parents are selected for you. The color of your skin, your religious background (or lack thereof) and, your country of origin, are all thrust upon you. Many good and bad characteristics come with this package. You have to work with what you've got.

But you have full control over the spiritual birth. Some of us become aware of our spiritual existence at an early age and some die as atheists. But to benefit from all that a spiritual life has to offer, we have to make a firm commitment in its progress.

On the concept of rebirth, 'Abdu'l-Bahá gave a beautiful explanation. He said:

> The rewards of this life are the virtues and perfections which adorn the reality of man. For example, he was dark and becomes luminous,

he was ignorant and becomes wise, he was neglectful and becomes vigilant, he was asleep and becomes awakened, he was dead and becomes living, he was blind and becomes a seer, he was deaf and becomes a hearer, he was earthly and becomes heavenly, he was material and becomes spiritual. Through these rewards he gains spiritual birth, and becomes a new creature. He becomes the manifestation of the verse in the Gospel where it is said of the disciples that they were born not of blood, nor of the will of the flesh, nor of the will of man, but of God; that is to say, they were delivered from the animal characteristics and qualities which are the characteristics of human nature, and they became qualified with the divine characteristics, which are the bounty of God; this is the meaning of the second birth. For such people there is no greater torture than being veiled from God, and no more severe punishment than sensual vices, dark qualities, lowness of nature, engrossment in carnal desires. When they are delivered through the light of faith from the darkness of these vices, and become illuminated with the radiance of the Sun of Reality, and ennobled with all the virtues, they esteem this the greatest reward, and they know it to be the true paradise.[8]

To those of us who have experienced a spiritual birth, life is lifted into a higher plane of existence. But the most glorious moment of this journey is when the Holy Spirit, the highest of all spirits in creation, touches the soul. At this stage the soul is re-created and lives in an intimate relationship with God. Just like many are ready to help a newborn, so is the Concourse on High waiting to rush to the aid of a searching soul, if it asks. The promise of this divine connection is none other than paradise. In fact, this is the prime goal of every religion. Unfortunately, in many cases this precious wisdom has been forgotten.

Reflection

For a moment think of your rebirth. Did it happen in one moment or a long period of time? Share it with us, if you wish.

Have you ever been touched by the Holy Spirit? What went through your mind to assure you that your experience was a significant connection to the divine?

Deeds (path of service)

Prayers and discussion of spiritual subjects give us an opportunity to immerse our souls in the divine realm and gain understanding of that reality. Yet, practicing what we learn or preach offers even greater enlightenment. One of the quotations that I like is this: "Say, O brethren! Let deeds, not words, be your adorning."[9]

In anything we do, whether it is learning how to swim, mastering physics, or becoming a writer, just reading books and listening to a teacher is not enough. One has to roll up one's sleeves and get one's hands dirty. It is only through action that we gain deeper understanding. Who would better understand love, compassion, or generosity than one who has practiced these qualities?

In the Holy Writings of all religions, a lot has been said about deeds. More importantly, we want participants to share their experiences, hoping that they will inspire other to achieve a higher level of service.

I think one of the greatest services we can render to our fellow humans is to help others in the spiritual path. It has been said that assisting a soul get one step closer to God is better than possessing the whole creation. How can we do this? There are many ways. One is to be patient with our friends, neighbors, colleagues, relatives, and strangers. What do you think?

CHAPTER 2

Knowledge of God

According to 'Abdu'l-Bahá, true spiritual awakening starts with the knowledge of God. How does one understand a Being so exalted, Whom no one has seen with the naked eye, yet Whose knowledge is spread out like the most beautiful tapestry throughout His creation? We do not learn about God the way we normally learn in class, through textbooks or lectures. There are at least four channels open to any soul, regardless of one's beliefs, to gain access to God. Let's first read Devine Words to quiet the mind and open the soul to higher understanding.

Devotion

☼

The Divine Messengers have been sent down, and their Books were revealed, for the purpose of promoting the knowledge of God, and of furthering unity and fellowship amongst men.[1]

☼

In the treasuries of the knowledge of God there lieth concealed a knowledge which, when applied, will largely, though not wholly, eliminate fear. This knowledge, however, should be taught from childhood, as it will greatly aid in its elimination. Whatever decreaseth fear increaseth courage.[2]

☼

Deeper Learning

As mentioned previously, one of the ways to receive the "merciful gifts and powers" of God is through knowing Him. According to Bahá'u'lláh, knowledge of God spans the entire creation, just like the sense of touch covers the whole body. Every object, seen or unseen, large or small, reflects one or more of God's attributes.

He said:

> From the exalted source, and out of the essence of His favor and bounty He hath entrusted every created thing with a sign of His knowledge...[3]

To speak about a subject so vast is to take a droplet from an ocean. The first and foremost step of an everlasting journey starts with knowing our Creator.

Learning is the gateway to knowledge, which is achieved through the faculty of understanding. One of the first lessons a newborn learns is how to take milk from his mother's breast. After this crucial moment, life continues as our appetite to understand translates into an endless discovery of this world. Recall how a two-year old can't stop asking questions, sometimes driving their parents crazy. This shows how gaining knowledge is an essential part of a human development; without it we face many challenges, some of them big enough to make living unbearably difficult.

Of all knowledge, discovering the purpose of life has been an age-old human quest. The answer is found in the short Bahá'í obligatory prayer. It begins like this: "I bear witness, O my God, that Thou hast created me to know Thee and to worship Thee."[4] In this sentence, one testifies to God's existence, acknowledging the awareness that springs from spiritual birth. One accepts that knowing God is the prime purpose of one's existence.

This answer to an age-old question may not necessarily sit well with some thinkers of our time, as they cannot accept a Creator Whom no one has seen with their naked eye. Many of them are intelligent professionals with superb credentials and awesome capacities to probe the workings of the universe, yet they have not witnessed the presence of God. At the same time billions others attest to the existence of a Divine Being. How come some "see" an invisible God, and others don't? Where is the missing link?

The gift of understanding is given to everyone, regardless of one's belief system. This gift "is none other except to enable His creature to know and recognize the one true God."[5] However the approach taken sometimes makes the difference between "seeing" the spiritual realm and being completely shut out from it. There are two kinds of understanding: that acquired through the mind, and that acquired through the heart. Through the mind we acquire the knowledge of the material world. But to probe into the invisible—God's realm—both mind and the heart are needed. God's message to a soul is: "Thy heart is My home; sanctify it for My descent."[6] The human heart, once cleansed, will be led to the Kingdom of God.

In addition to the knowledge of the purpose of creation, we also need to discover our true nature. According to the Bible, "God created man to be immortal, and made him to be an image of his own."[7] In the Old Testament, God has said, "Let us make man in our image, after our likeness."[8] The same idea is reiterated in many of Bahá'u'lláh's Writings. He explains that when the Scriptures speak of God's image being engraved upon us, the meaning is that the "Names and attributes" of God are part of our innermost being. The following four ideas explain this reality in greater depth:

1. The spheres in which God and humanity exist are distinct and separate. God the Creator cannot be part of

His own creation. For example, an artist is distinctly separate from her artwork. Though paintings reflect many of the painter's attributes, they never live in each other's domain. A portrait will never become its painter.

2. Though we are created in God's image, one should not conclude that God has a physical form like humans. It is our spirit that is made in God's image. Our powers are limited yet God is beyond any constraint.

3. When born, the goodness we inherit is in potential, just as a mighty tree is latent in a seed. We are noble beings: within us is enshrined the capacity and responsibility to reflect the beauty of God. This does not happen automatically, as we all know too well. The right education and environment is required as well as constant effort if one is to blossom into a beautiful spirit. This is a goal within everyone's reach.

4. Each of us is endowed with free will. The choices we make can sometimes lead us astray from God's plan to know and worship Him. Some commit crimes, murders, and other atrocious acts. Yet the image of God remains stamped upon their beings. For them there is always hope of change, if only they make the effort. Free will holds us accountable for our actions.

How can we increase our knowledge of God? The first is through the portal of self. As mentioned before, right from our first moment of existence we must grow in order to cope with life. Growth never stops. Our physical, intellectual, emotional, and spiritual well-being all depend on a never-ending journey of discovery.

In addition to our capacities, the relationships we develop are a foundation of life. Our first relationships are with our mother, father and siblings. Later we get to know friends, neighbors, teachers, co-workers, a spouse, children and grandchildren. Life becomes an expansion of human experience. Some relationships we choose, some are thrust upon us, and others we discard. Our interactions with others provide opportunities to gain a better understanding of qualities such as love, trust, patience, kindness and forgiveness. When a conscious effort is made to turn our attention towards divine attributes rather than seeking vices, the self transforms itself from potential to reality. Step by step, it grows closer to the Divine Self. According to 'Abdu'l-Bahá:

> …With the human soul…Its only movement is towards perfection…Divine perfection is

infinite, therefore the progress of the soul is also infinite.[9]

What are the processes of perfection? Let's consider a mirror. When it is turned towards the sun, it reflects light. If it is kept in the darkness, it will reflect nothing. Also, if the mirror is dirty, although turned towards the sun, it will reflect only some of the light. Similar to a mirror, when the soul turns towards God and ponders His attributes, it will come to reflect many facets of goodness. The cleaner the soul, through the development of virtues, the more it will see in it the reflection of God's beauty.

The second way to gain knowledge of God is through His Manifestations. According to recorded history some of them are Adam, Abraham, Krishna, Zoroaster, Buddha, Moses, Jesus, Mohammad, the Báb and Bahá'u'lláh. They are direct links between God and us. Though they appear in this world in human form, these Beings are different from us in many ways. Here are four important points to remember:

Unlike ordinary humans, they are perfect Beings who reflect all the attributes of God. They are perfect mirrors. According to Bahá'u'lláh, God "...hath ordained the knowledge of these sanctified Beings to be identical with the knowledge of His own Self."[10]

Each brings a divine message for the age in which they appear. Unfortunately, with passage of time the pure heavenly water they shower over mankind is muddied through misunderstandings, corruptions and dogmas. Each time a Manifestation appears on Earth, He first refreshes the spiritual teachings by adding, changing or removing laws and practices of previous religions, according the capacity and needs of the people. Divine Revelation helps souls move closer to their Creator, promotes unity and concord, and allows civilization to advance materially and spiritually. Religious rituals and traditions, when they lose the light of truth and are reduced to outer forms, can become barriers, limiting people from recognizing God's Manifestations. The essence of all religions, their spiritual teachings, is the same. For example, kindness, generosity and compassion are not only for Christians: they are part of the core beliefs of all religions.

These Manifestations bring social laws based on the needs of the time, so that civilization can flourish and humans can live in harmony. Every time these Educators appear, through their examples and words we reach a higher plane of understanding of God. Reading the Holy Words is essential as they are filled with inspiration and guidance. The soul is soothed to know more about why and how it is created, and that knowledge can only come from the Creator through His Manifestations.

All the scriptures mention and glorify the names of God repeatedly. For example, in Qur'án there over one hundred unique divine attributes mentioned. It declares God as merciful, compassionate, mighty, wise, knowing, and clement. In the Bible it is said: "God is light, and in him is no darkness at all."

In the Writings of Bahá'u'lláh, the Báb, and 'Abdu'l-Bahá, the attributes of God are frequently mentioned. Many of their prayers start with God's glorification and end with mention of His names. Some of these names from Bahá'u'lláh's Writings include: the All-Perceiving, the Exalted, the All-Merciful, the Knower of things unseen, the Most Holy, the All-Praised, the Great Giver, the Ever-Forgiving, the Most Powerful, and the Most Compassionate.

We are familiar with these attributes though we may not be part of a religion, as we have had to deal with them in our daily lives. For example, as a victim, we have had to deal with whether to forgive or avenge the wrongdoings of others. Suffering makes us think long and hard. Can we be ever-forgiving, as God is? In other words, do we have the capacity to pardon the actions of others, no matter how unjust? In fact, the sole survivor of a rampage in which her husband and four children died not only forgave the killer but also prayed for him. The Scriptures teach us to dig deeper and not be satisfied with superficial practice of any divine attribute. For example, it is easy to love a friend or a family member, but would you love someone who has harmed you? Would you love an enemy? Would love someone who has brutally murdered a loved one of yours? According to the Holy Books, God's love encompasses every person. For an ever-forgiving God, forgiving any wrong, regardless of the severity, is not out of the question. There is great merit in choosing the high road: in doing so we align ourselves with God's knowledge. All religions are springs of fresh wisdom that carry yearning souls closer to their Beloved and help them detach from the transitory things of this world.

The third source of God's knowledge is the Holy Spirit. Understanding the link between God and the Holy Spirit is vitally important. God is separate from His creation and there is no direct connection between the absolute and contingent world except through the intervention of the Holy Spirit, the Great Spirit, the "breath" of God. God is like the sun and the Holy Spirit is like the rays of the sun. We need the sun to survive, but if we were to approach it too closely, we would be consumed in its heat. Likewise, if the sun came down to us, the earth would be incinerated. The rays of the sun carry the light and the heat of the sun. God's power is channeled through the Holy Spirit.

The Manifestations obey the promptings of the same Spirit. For Moses this Spirit was symbolized in the form of a burning bush, for Jesus a dove, for Muhammad Gabriel and for Bahá'u'lláh the Maid of Heaven. Manifestations are not schooled like the rest of us: they possess an innate knowledge. The Holy Spirit instructs them, to the extent that every moment of their lives, whatever they say or do is a consequence of their obedience to the Holy Spirit.

Humans also feel the power of the Holy Spirit. 'Abdu'l-Bahá explains:

> Today the light of Truth is shining upon the world in its abundance; the breezes of the heavenly garden are blowing throughout all regions; the call of the Kingdom is heard in all lands, and the breath of the Holy Spirit is felt in all hearts that are faithful.[12]

To receive the divine bounties available to the faithful ones, we must be continually receptive to them. The good news is that the outpouring of these blessings is continuous and abundant. All we have to do is turn our antenna in the right direction.

According to 'Abdu'l-Bahá, the Holy Spirit transforms our living conditions, regardless of our beliefs. It removes strife and wars so that humans may unite. All the wonders of this age, manifested in new sciences and arts, in an emerging a global consciousness, a new awakening in human rights, and the pursuit of justice are all inspirations of the Holy Spirit. No human development can happen without this force. 'Abdu'l-Bahá assures us that the future is so bright that the Most Great Peace will surely come, powered by the mercy of God and channeled through the Holy Spirit.

To tie these four types of existence—Divinity, the Holy Spirit, the Manifestations of God and human beings—into an array of cosmic connectivity, we turn to the Bahá'í ring symbol. The kingdom of God is at the top, below is the realm of the Manifestations and the third existence is humanity. A line cutting across all these three realities is the Holy Spirit.

The fourth way we learn about God is through our environment. If we are lucky, we are greeted with loving, kind, patient, and generous parents. If our star shines even brighter we come across loyal friends, compassionate bosses, and live in a kinder and gentler society. The environment is a laboratory to learn about these virtues.

Not everyone is so lucky all the time. Spiritual travel is filled with mishaps and confusion. Sometimes the path looks extremely bleak. You don't feel the presence of God in your life. But regardless of your spiritual state, God is still watching you as He always does, according to Bahá'u'lláh's words:

> Consider, moreover, how frequently doth man become forgetful of his own self, whilst God remaineth, through His all-encompassing knowledge, aware of His creature, and continueth to shed upon him the manifest radiance of His glory. It is evident, therefore, that, in such circumstances, He is closer to him than his own self. He will, indeed, so remain forever, for, whereas the one true God knoweth all things, perceiveth all things, and comprehendeth all things, mortal man is prone to err, and is ignorant of the mysteries that lie enfolded within him...[13]

If you feel remote from Him, who has moved? It's always you. In times of remoteness from the Divine Presence, examine your spiritual account. Seek to pick up the broken pieces, put them back together and fly again. Keep in mind that we are always under the watchful eyes of God. He sees us through His kind, generous and compassionate eyes, just as loving parents see their children.

When we do manage to show forth the names and attributes of God, we have entered the phase of re-creating ourselves as beautiful souls. When we struggle to reflect the attributes of God, when it is hard for us to love or to forgive, we gain insight into God's name the All-Loving or the Ever-Forgiving. This is a type of knowledge of God. To realize this divine process in this day is also o also fulfill an ancient prophecy. During the last few decades, many have predicted the end of the world on specific days, when the dead would literally rise from their graves and enter heaven in rapture. Raptures that were supposed to take place in 2000 and 2011 did not come to pass. According to Bahá'u'lláh, awakening is not a one-day event. Rather, the dead are quickened by the Holy Spirit every day and will continue to do so for centuries to come. He explains:

> For he who had believed in God and in the Manifestation of His beauty was raised from the grave of heedlessness, gathered together in

the sacred ground of the heart, quickened to the life of faith and certitude, and admitted into the paradise of the divine presence. What paradise can be loftier than this?[14]

Returning to the short Bahá'í obligatory prayer, we can now see that enshrined in its affirmation of our purpose—to know and to worship God—is the love of God to be explored in the next chapter.

Reflection

Reflect on all the virtues within you and come up with four lists:

Developed virtues: In this category you put all your best qualities, the ones in which you are the strongest. Some examples would be kindness, intelligence, or generosity. These are your very best, the ones with which your friends and family identify you.

Virtues needed development: List the qualities you have problems with. For me, patience is always a problem, which can cause friction within me and with my relationships with others, including God.

Desired virtues: The wish list. Qualities that you would like to work on.

Bonus virtues: The qualities that you always had. You did not have to struggle for them. They come so naturally to you. For me, it is compassion. Since childhood, my heart leaps out whenever I find someone needs help. If I had all the power of the world, there would be no suffering anywhere on earth. (I know that divine wisdom does not allow total paradise, else we would all become spiritually lazy!)

Some of us have a problem worshiping God. Do you have this issue? If so, why do you think you do? Consider that worship is more than just praying in churches, temples, or synagogues. Every moment of your life can be an act of worship.

Deeds (path of service)

You must become the means of lighting the world of humanity. This is the infallible proof and sign. Every progress depends on two things, knowledge and practice. First acquire knowledge, and, when conviction is reached, put it into practice.[15]

CHAPTER 3

Love of God

Loving another human being is as common as eating a meal, yet discovering how to love God is not easy. There are obstacles, some which may seem insurmountable. If you do discover the love of God, what is its highest level? We'll explore this very important question.

Devotion

For the love of God, and them that serve Him, arise to aid this sublime and momentous Revelation. Religious fanaticism and hatred are a world-devouring fire, whose violence none can quench. The Hand of Divine power can, alone, deliver mankind from this desolating affliction. Consider the war that hath involved the two Nations, how both sides have renounced their possessions and their lives. How many the villages that were completely wiped out![1]

☼

But as it is written, Eye hath not seen, nor ear heard, neither have entered into the heart of man, the things which God hath prepared for them that love him.[2]

☼

Deeper Learning

Think for a moment of all the people you admire: your heroes. They could be your parents, your children, your spouse, a friend, a neighbor, a teacher, and even someone you have never met. What is the common bond in all of these relationships? Isn't it an emotional and spiritual connection that causes your fascination for them to grow? You want to know everything about them: you hang on their every word; you help them in difficulties and even confide in them. Adoration for your heroes is a result of a love that you have for them. It is a selfless attraction to a person, object or idea: to know and to love are inseparable. Love is manifested at all levels of our existence. Even before we take our first breath, we are immersed in our parents' love. Every atom, molecule, cell, and organ obeys the law of cohesion to form a whole. Our bodies stay close to the Earth's surface by the pull of gravitational force. Human interactions are governed by the degree of love we feel for others. The pursuit of art, science, business, and hobbies are all highly driven by passion.

Without the force of love, disintegration is sure to come. After death, the attraction of elements disappears and the body begins to decay until all the organs, cells and molecules break down into their simplest forms. Lack of love at a social level leads to the breakdown of friendships, families, and societies.

What is love? How can one define the unseen and immeasurable? Though love has been discussed, examined, and glorified in thousands of books, yet our human capacity to understand this emotion in all of its aspects is limited. One thing is clear, however: the tenderness of love is felt in the heart. This is true whether love be for a person, an idea, or God. Love is as vast and as complicated as creation itself; no one can confine it to words. Yet let us consider the subject of love, the cause of our existence. Living without love is like living without sunshine.

In the previous section we looked at the knowledge of God. But no one can truly know God without love. In the Bible it is said: "He that loveth not knoweth not God; for God is love."[3] Whatever I mention here about love is only a drop in an ocean.

To better understand this most essential power, I did a quick survey of several religions and discovered, as expected, that love is the central theme in every tradition. In Buddhism, God is not specifically mentioned, yet love is at the heart of wisdom from world religious. In *The Eightfold Path*, one of the Buddha's principal teachings of enlightenment, it is said: "He has cast away ill-will; he dwells with a heart free from ill-will; cherishing love and compassion toward all living beings, he cleanses his heart from ill-will."[4]

In Judaism it is said: "Let all those that seek Thee rejoice and be glad in Thee; and let such as love Thy salvation say continually: 'Let God be magnified.'"[5]

The theme of love is expanded on to such a degree in Christianity that it is considered one of the pillars of the religion. Jesus explains how the Unseen can be brought closer to us through love: "No man hath seen God at any time. If we love one another, God dwelleth in us, and his love is perfected in us.[6]

In the *Qur'án*, it is said, "Yet are there some amongst mankind who take to themselves peers other than God; they love them as they should love God while those who believe love God more."[7]

When I examined love in the Bahá'í Writings, it was as if entering an enormous storehouse. A search for the word "love" in the Ocean program, a database of religious texts, yielded 8889 hits in 519 documents. In the Bahá'í Faith, the concept of love is like a diamond with a multitude of facets. Among the things I learned were:

- An individual may relate to love in many ways.
- Knowledge cannot be acquired without love for the object of understanding.

- Faith is directly tied to love (the subject of the next section).
- Justice cannot exist without love.
- The unity of mankind, one of the prime principles of the Bahá'í Faith, will not happen without the love of God and of our fellow human beings.
- The growth of the Faith, an ongoing concern since the day the Báb declared His revelation, requires love.
- The divine lamp found in every soul cannot be kindled without love.
- Love is the key to the spiritual recovery of a sick soul.
- Work is only considered worship if it is done with love.
- Lasting changes on an individual or societal level cannot take place without love.

These few examples barely scratch the surface of a subject as vast and deep as the universe. The Bahá'í Writings are a well-spring from which flows limitless understandings of love.

'Abdu'l-Bahá, as recorded in *Paris Talks*, explains four kinds of love, the first of which is God's love for man.

While reflecting on this type of love, the sun came to my mind. Every species on earth is dependent on the sun's light and heat for its survival and growth. Every mineral, plant, animal, and human receives a share according to its needs. If the sun were to be cut off, life of every kind would face annihilation and our planet would become barren like Mars. In the same way, the Sun of Reality is the cause of our existence and our sustainer. In the invisible world, man's love and attraction to God is the reason for the uninterrupted progress of human life.

Love flows from the soul to its Creator only when a spiritual birth has taken place, as was discussed previously. No one is forced into this relationship; rather it is a conscious effort on the part of a soul, undertaken through free will, to establish a relationship with Divinity. This soul begins to see the Beauty of God with new eyes and approaches paradise according to his own capacities.

'Abdu'l-Bahá also discusses a third kind of love:

The third is the love of God towards the Self or Identity of God. This is the transfiguration of His beauty, the reflection of Himself in the mirror of His Creation. This is the reality of love, the Ancient Love, the Eternal Love. Through one ray of this Love all other love exists.[8]

God spreads His knowledge through His creation, the most exquisite tapestry of His attributes and names. Knowledge, love and beauty come together to generate the most magnificent fruit of creativity.

'Abdu'l-Bahá continues:

The fourth is the love of man for man. The love which exists between the hearts of believers is prompted by the ideal of the unity of spirits. This love is attained through the knowledge of God, so that men see the Divine Love reflected in the heart. Each sees in the other the Beauty of God reflected in the soul, and finding this point of similarity, they are attracted to one another in love. This love will make all men the waves of one sea, this love will make them all the stars of one heaven and the fruits of one tree. This love will bring the realization of true accord, the foundation of real unity.[9]

We are all familiar with this kind of love. In order to demonstrate this love, we must understand our true nature, that we are created noble and in the image of the Most Glorious. When we see the same image in others, we are drawn to them in a bond of love. Finally, the realization that we are drops of the same ocean dawns upon us. When this idea grows into a global consciousness, the concept of "us and them" evaporates, and is replaced with a consciousness of the oneness of humanity. To love and be loved by others and to treat them as we would like to be treated is the golden rule of every religion. Our love for our fellow human beings can transform our current world into paradise: The Golden Age. This is God's promise to us.

Love has received considerable attention outside of religion, too. It has been well-studied and researched throughout history. Writers, philosophers, poets, scientists, and educators have incessantly explored love and its many implications. Shakespeare, the renowned English playwright's most famous romantic work was *Romeo and Juliet*, which celebrates the passion of two young lovers. In the East there is a similar love story called *Laila and Majnun*. Countless novels, paintings and poems are dedicated to love. Somewhere in the plot of every Hollywood and Bollywood movie lies a love story. The Taj Mahal, a mausoleum renowned worldwide for its architectural magnificence and aesthetic beauty, built by Shah Jahan, an emperor of 17th century India, symbolizes the everlasting love he had for his wife, Mumtaz Mahal. Millions visit it annually.

The following story is an example of love between a daughter and father. A man punished his three-year old daughter for wasting a roll of gold wrapping paper. Money was tight, and he became infuriated when the child tried to decorate a box to put under the tree. Nevertheless, the little girl brought the gift to her father the next morning and said, "This is for you, Daddy." He was embarrassed by his earlier overreaction, but his anger flared again when he found that the box was empty. He yelled at her, "Don't you know that when you give someone a present, there's supposed to be something inside of it?" The little girl looked up at him with tears in her eyes and said, "Oh, Daddy it's not empty. I blew kisses into the box. All for you, Daddy." The father was crushed. He put his arms around his little girl, and begged her for forgiveness. He kept that gold box by his bed for years. Whenever he was discouraged, he would take out an imaginary kiss and remember the love of the child who had put it there. In a very real sense, each of us has been given a gold container filled with unconditional love and kisses. There is not a more precious possession anyone could have.

Human love comes in many shades. There is romantic love, love for your country and love for your religion. Love drives passion in us, but it can be blind. It can betray us and lead us astray into destruction. Worst of all, when love becomes obsession, it is an obstacle in the spiritual path. Love has led many to disagreement, disunity, and violence. Passion is a good thing but it must be tempered with cool-mindedness.

What is the highest expression of love? In my opinion, it is sacrifice, the act of giving up a prized possession for the sake of something that has a higher, or more worthy claim. Religious rituals and traditions are filled with many examples of worshippers offering goods to God. In the Bible, God commanded Abraham to sacrifice His son, Isaac. Obedient to this divine request, the prophet travelled with his son for three days until he reached the spot that God directed Him towards. Just as Abraham was about to sacrifice His son, he was prevented by an angel: a ram appeared, which Abraham sacrificed instead of his son.

When Bahá'u'lláh, His family, and His followers were confined in prison in Akka, His son Mirza Mihdi used to pray on the roof, pacing back and forth as he chanted. One evening he was so immersed in prayer that he fell through an open skylight and was fatally wounded. In the face of death, his Father asked him if he would like to be cured of his injuries. However, Mirza Mihdi wished to sacrifice His life so that the authorities would allow the pilgrims, who travelled from afar to see Bahá'u'lláh, to attain their hearts' desire. The death of Mirza Mihdi, also known as the Purest Branch, was regarded by Bahá'u'lláh as His own sacrifice.

A lover's greatest desire is to sacrifice for his Beloved. When this yearning is fulfilled, the insistent self evaporates in the face of a higher Being. This is bliss. The love and sacrifice that the Manifestations of God demonstrate to their Creator are the best examples history can provide. The lives of Abraham, Moses, Buddha, Krishna, Christ, Muhammad, the Báb and Bahá'u'lláh are all sterling examples of love and sacrifice. The Báb, Who was martyred in a public square in Iran, longed to shed His blood for His Beloved. He said:

> O Remnant of God, I am wholly sacrificed to Thee; I am content with curses in Thy way; I crave naught but to be slain in Thy love; and God the Supreme sufficeth as an Eternal Protection.[10]

It is my hope that this very brief presentation on the love of God will cause us to consider how this love influences our lives. In the next chapter, we will discover how the love of God cannot exist in one's heart without faith.

Reflection

What does love mean to you? What are some of the challenges in understanding and showing these four kinds of love? The Bahá'í Faith aims to bring about the unity of mankind. The dynamic that exists between love and unity is worthy of exploration: "The more love is expressed among mankind and the stronger the power of unity, the greater will be this reflection and revelation, for the greatest bestowal of God is love. Love is the source of all the bestowals of God. Until love takes possession of the heart no other divine bounty can be revealed in it."[11]

Through love comes power of unity. What are other gifts and powers that are nurtured through love?

Deeds (path of service)

In this Revelation the hosts which can render it victorious are the hosts of praiseworthy deeds and upright character.[12]

There is a strong connection between love and deeds. Love of any kind—whether it is for our parents, family, country, friend, and spouse—should lead us to action. Saying, "I love you," is never enough. Parenting is a good example. If one is to successfully raise a family, one must be prepared to make many sacrifices. The quality of care and sacrifice shows the depth of one's love for family members.

> It is incumbent upon thee to summon the people, under all conditions, to whatever will cause them to show forth spiritual characteristics and goodly deeds, so that all may become aware of that which is the cause of human upliftment, and may, with the utmost endeavor, direct themselves towards the most sublime Station and the Pinnacle of Glory. 13

One can think of many things that will lead to human upliftment. One of the most challenging is to love all mankind. In contrast, caring for our family or ethnic group is far easier. How do we love everyone on this planet to the extent that we care for their wellbeing? Some might think such is not attainable, but Bahá'ís believe it is possible. What are some of the obstacles that must be overcome?

CHAPTER 4

Spirit of Faith

Faith, like knowledge and love, is the foundation of human existence. Without it, life is not worth much. When we climb to the highest rung on the ladder of faith—faith in God—a metamorphosis takes place just like a caterpillar transforms into a beautiful monarch butterfly. But for the soul, hanging on to the cord of steadfastness is not easy. There is a steep penalty to pay in losing faith in God—in not reaching the "blissful abode." How do we manage this risk?

Devotion

> That the divers communions of the earth, and the manifold systems of religious belief, should never be allowed to foster the feelings of

animosity among men, is, in this Day, of the essence of the Faith of God and His Religion.[1]

☼

The voice of the true Faith calleth aloud, at this moment, and saith: O people! Verily, the Day is come, and My Lord hath made Me to shine forth with a light whose splendor hath eclipsed the suns of utterance. Fear ye the Merciful, and be not of them that have gone astray.[2]

☼

Deeper Learning

Regarding the spirit of faith, 'Abdu'l-Bahá said:

...the magnet of faith and service is the manifested loving power of the spirit of faith. It allows one to attract the divine virtues and to experience spiritual happiness. The key is a life of faith. We must endeavor to know ourselves, for within each of us lies mysteries of existence. Then, we can enter the Kingdom revealed and feel the healing warmth of the Sun of Reality.[3]

In this brief excerpt, there are many important points to consider. Two of them are attraction to divine virtues and spiritual happiness, both of which are themes that we'll regularly visit in this course. The third is faith, the understanding and growth of which is of the highest importance because it leads us to virtues and happiness.

What is faith? If you ask people, you will get different answers depending on experience, age, belief and knowledge. Let's look at some of the more common understandings of faith. There is no doubt that faith is the foundation of life–but as we examine various ways of seeing faith, make sure to reflect on your own system of belief. Through it, self-knowledge will certainly grow, as promised in the previous quotations, and lead us to discovery of the mysteries enshrined within us. Faith is like a compass that guides a wise spiritual traveler on the path of self-discovery, and with every new insight the soul inches closer to paradise.

Faith has many meanings and definitions. Let's look at four of them.

One meaning of faith is confidence or trust in a person or thing. Our earliest experience of trust in another human being occurs during the first few days of life. The newborn immediately senses the love of the mother and starts to trust her. Have you noticed that in crisis—it could be pain, hunger or fear—where a newborn turns for comfort? It always seeks relief in mother's arms, nowhere else. As faith in the mother grows, the young one gradually learns to trust others. Faith is extended to others, starting with the child's father and siblings.

When this faith does not exist, what happens? One becomes reclusive, shy and hopeless. Just as oxygen and water are essential for physical existence, our emotional well-being depends upon faith. Just imagine parents and children living with little or no faith among each other. Such a family will surely be dysfunctional and may even disintegrate. We see similar effects on a larger scale, too. Since the summer of 2011, ongoing convulsions in the Middle East, protests in Europe, and riots in England, all reflect a lack of faith in political leaders.

The kind of faith of which we've been speaking is born of knowledge and trust (a derivative of love), key building blocks for the lives of individuals, families, societies, and the world. Would you allow a surgeon to perform a heart transplant on you if you knew he was incompetent? Would a construction worker climb a scaffold known to be unsafe? Obviously not! Faith doesn't just cement relationships. It is fundamental to our survival!

A second type of faith involves adherence to a code of ethics. A shared commitment to a common set of values helps to cement trust in the integrity of the group's members.

The third type of faith is a system of religious belief, such Bahá'í Faith, Hindu Faith or Jewish Faith. Membership in a religious community can provide comfort and a sense of belonging but doesn't necessarily include an awareness of God. (I had that experience myself.)

Finally, faith can mean a belief that is not proof-based, such as acceptance of a Creator whom no one has seen. This faith is born of an intimate relationship between the soul and the Holy Spirit as discussed before. As the relationship grows, so do one's inner powers. Let's look deeper into this faith.

According to 'Abdu'l-Bahá, "The first sign of faith is love."[4] In human relationships we deal with visible faces, but in a divine engagement we travel into the unknown. Moreover, this is a journey for which we must take personal responsibility. "For the faith of no man can be conditioned by anyone except himself."[5] Our beliefs require us to be accountable for every action we take.

Faith requires trust. Consider the life of a blind person. For her, tasks sighted people take for granted become difficult, even dangerous. Walking to a neighbor's house, she could run into objects or other people, trip over bad cracks in the sidewalk, fall down a step, or even walk out in front of an oncoming car. Fortunately, she can learn to deal with these obstacles in a variety of ways. For example, she could get a guide dog. But just any dog won't do. It must be a dog that has been carefully trained, and then she must learn to work with and trust her new canine friend. She learns to trust her guide dog through experience: it leads her safely through her day. Thus, knowledge leads to trust, which blossoms into faith.

This is a metaphor for our spiritual life. Sometimes our inner vision is blurry. We may stand at a fork in the road, unable to clearly see which branch to take. Or we may be called upon to undertake some task without knowing exactly where it will lead. In the Bahá'í Faith, for example, we are called upon to teach others about Bahá'u'lláh. Some undertake the journey into the unknown through obedience to higher authorities, such as the Central Figures, the Guardian, or the Universal House of Justice. Our history is replete with inspirational stories of heroic deeds accomplished through faith and knowledge. When individuals take the first step, divine assistance comes. Think of the great travel teachers and pioneers who selflessly moved around the world and those martyrs who gave up their lives for the love of God.

One such example is the remarkable life of Martha Root. She was called the "archetype of Bahá'í teachers" by the Guardian. After she became a Bahá'í in 1909, she had two private interviews with 'Abdu'l-Bahá during His visit to America and Canada. Fascinated by the simplicity and majesty of the Faith, this small-framed woman from an ordinary family in Cambridgeboro, Pennsylvania, decided to explore Bahá'í communities around the world. In 1915, she started her global journey alone with the hope of financing her travels as a journalist. She visited Egypt, India, Burma, Japan,

Hawaii, and finally returned to the USA. She met Bahá'ís wherever possible. Her great regret was that she could not enter Haifa to visit the Master, as the region was engulfed in conflict during that time. In 1919, Martha Root undertook another world voyage, this time fuelled by the idea of sharing the gems of Bahá'u'lláh's Message with the world. In the course of her travels, she reached millions through her newspaper articles and radio broadcasts. She met with common people as well as kings and queens, scholars, and other prominent leaders. Among those whom she met was Queen Marie of Romania (who eventually became a Bahá'í), and president of Czechoslovakia and Nobel-prize-winning poet Rabindranath Tagore. Was it easy? Not at all! She worried about her limitations and suffered from fatigue and cancer. She was neither strong, rich, nor attractive by the standards of her times. Often she was in great danger. Whenever she was downhearted, she read the counsels of 'Abdu'l-Bahá and more importantly, she prayed for greater capacity to serve more intelligently and lovingly. Traveling alone and mostly in male-dominated society, Martha Root encountered many challenges yet she was careful not to become a barrier between any soul and the Message of Bahá'u'lláh.

Regardless of what stage of growth you are at, your faith can be at risk. Once you profess your belief in Bahá'u'lláh, there is no guarantee that you will maintain it. Perhaps you or someone you know has experienced this. Many losing faith in God, for our faith is tested over and over again. The closer you are to God, the greater the tests become. When faced with persecution by the Romans, the disciples of Jesus Christ started to lose their faith in their Savior. Mary Magdalene, the strongest of them all, saved them during this difficult time. Many join the Faith with great enthusiasm and expectation, but when difficulty or disappointment creeps in, slowly their steadfastness withers away. Why? Could it be that they allow trivial issues become more important to them than the love of God?

How do we keep our faith strong and healthy? By keeping the love of God at the center of our lives. We must work to maintaining our relationship with God, realizing that as we grow closer to the Divine Presence our faith grows stronger only by overcoming tests and difficulties. Focus and balance are two key elements.

Think of a tightrope walker at a circus, working without a net. To successfully cross from one end to the other of the tensioned wire, he must maintain his balance. Failure means serious injury. To attain the level of skill and confidence required for success, he must put in long hours of practice. Likewise, in our spiritual path we must learn to focus on our relationship with God. Maintaining a balanced life is always a challenge, as this material existence is filled with distractions that can lead us to barter God's bounty for the benefits of this world.

For example, a man interested in the Bahá'í Faith approached a priest for a "second opinion" on the new religion. He offered the priest a few books on the Faith and asked him to comment on them. The priest refused. The man was disturbed by his reaction. He really wanted to get an opinion from someone he trusted. When pressed for a reason for his refusal, the clergyman said, "What if this religion is true? Son, being a priest is all I have known for most of my life. Changing religions means losing everything that I have—a profession. I am too old to start all over again."

In 1899, it is reported that 'Abdu'l-Bahá gave a commandment to the first western pilgrim as part of His parting address. He said:

> As ye have faith so shall your powers and blessings be. This is the balance -- this is the balance -- this is the balance.[6]

If we maintain our faith, the promise of God's bounty is unimaginably wonderful according to 'Abdu'l-Bahá. He said:

> Your Lord hath assuredly promised His servants who are firm and steadfast to render them victorious at all times, to exalt their word, propagate their power, diffuse their lights, strengthen their hearts, elevate their banners, assist their hosts, brighten their stars, increase the abundance of the showers of mercy upon them, and enable the brave lions to conquer.[7]

The life of Martha Root is a living proof of the Master's words. She wasn't called the "lioness at the

Threshold" for nothing! With all the powers unleashed in this Day of God, anyone can do extraordinary deeds. This is the age of fulfillment in which the poor shall inherit the earth, only if one should arise.

The tests and difficulties that come in believing in the Revelation of Bahá'u'lláh should not be underestimated. In our awesome journey to paradise, tests and difficulties in successive turns will surely visit each one of us. In the Qur'an it is said: "Never will they attain (unto Divine bounty), except through severe trials."[8] Yet for the people of faith, trials, tribulations, disasters, sorrow, pain and illness are all parts of the spiritual path of purification that they travel as they draw closer to God, hoping ultimately to attain His Presence.

If Bahá'ís don't cling to the cord of steadfastness, what is their loss? Paradise? More than that! Consider these Words of Bahá'u'lláh:

> Put away the cups of Paradise and all the life-giving waters they contain, for lo, the people of Bahá have entered the blissful abode of the Divine Presence, and quaffed the wine of

reunion, from the chalice of the beauty of their Lord, the All-Possessing, the Most High.[9]

Reflection

Have you ever thought of what it is like to be truly happy? How do happiness and faith tie together?

There is a connection between love and faith. Can you recall the first time you recognized that relationship?

On the ladder of faith, what is the highest rung? I think it is certitude. What do you think?

Deeds (path of service)

> Strive thou, that haply thou mayest achieve a deed the fragrance of which shall never fade from the earth.[10]

What sort of deed could that be? Just "a deed" could leave an everlasting footprint in this material world. What a wonderful thought!

> We have admonished Our loved ones to fear God, a fear which is the fountain-head of all goodly deeds and virtues. It is the commander of the hosts of justice in the city of Bahá. Happy the man that hath entered the shadow of its luminous standard, and laid fast hold thereon. He, verily, is of the Companions of the Crimson Ark, which hath been mentioned in the Qayyum-i-Asma.[11]

Fear of God has been mentioned in scriptures of all religions. As indicated in this extract, it can lead us to good deeds and the pursuit of virtues. Our instinct is to run away from anything that causes us fear. How do we reconcile these opposing emotions?

> Say: O people of God! Adorn your temples with the adornment of trustworthiness and piety. Help, then, your Lord with the hosts of goodly deeds and a praiseworthy character. We have forbidden you dissension and conflict in My Books, and My Scriptures, and My Scrolls, and My Tablets, and have wished thereby

naught else save your exaltation and advancement.[12]

In the last chapter we saw that the fear of God can motivate us to perform good deeds and develop virtues. In this quotation, there is a connection between trustworthiness and deeds. More interestingly, we are asked to help our "Lord with the hosts of goodly deeds and a praiseworthy character." Does the spirit of faith have anything to do with your path of service?

CHAPTER 5

Philanthropic Deeds

A common theme in the messages of Universal House of Justice is for the believers to find their paths of service, ways to engage in building a neighborhood and become the catalyst of change in society. Similar divine guidance echoed through the words of 'Abdu'l-Bahá one hundred years ago when He travelled in North America. He said that through philanthropic deeds, one can obtain "merciful gifts and powers."

A quick study shows that the human desire to help our brothers and sisters is alive and healthy. Look beyond the headlines and you will find a mighty river of generosity flowing towards the needy, poor and sick and filling their hearts with hope. It is happening in places close to home and in the far corners of the world. The philanthropic movement is so vast and enduring that it boggles the minds of most pessimists. The wealthy, poor and educated are all part of this phenomenon. Bahá'ís can connect with these like-minded citizens in building a new world order.

Devotion

☼

Say, O brethren! Let deeds, not words, be your adorning.[1]

☼

We have decreed that war shall be waged in the path of God with the armies of wisdom and utterance, and of a goodly character and praiseworthy deeds.[2]

☼

Deeper Learning

Philanthropic deeds are the fourth way to obtain "merciful gifts and powers" in our awesome spiritual journey. Let's start with deeds. What is a deed? It's the act of doing something, like performing a task or achieving a goal in a measurable, concrete way. Through such actions, whether they are daily chores, service to others, or your occupation, your character is reflected through the deeds you perform. If you simply do or say nothing, no one, including yourself, will know your true capacities. When we do things well, it gives us confidence and adds to our treasure house of experience. More importantly, our deeds can serve as a measure of our capacities. Even our failures have value, giving us opportunities to improve our skills. Imagine a one-year old learning how to walk. At first the child may hold an adult's hand or hang onto furniture as she tries to walk. She falls often, but the day comes when she achieves balance and strength and is able to confidently stand on her own. In the same way, repeated effort is the only way to increase self-knowledge. Moreover, deeds are not undertaken: they grow out of and interact with other aspects of our inmost being, such as knowledge, love and faith.

For example, suppose you want to learn how to swim, which I did when I was forty years old. Ultimately, there is no way to learn to swim other than getting into the water and practicing the basic skills required. But just getting into the water can be a challenge. Often people who can't swim fear the water and don't trust their own abilities. So learning to swim is also about trusting yourself and your teacher, and about developing faith and confidence that you can safely enjoy your time in the water. Without this faith, it is hard to learn much of anything. With it, a love of the water often blossoms, and through practice and perseverance, you will learn how to float, breath properly, and move your arms and legs in concert. In short, you will become a swimmer! Knowledge, love, faith, and action come together to make this happen.

Or consider the example of Terry Fox, a Canadian suffering from bone cancer who decided to embark upon a unique challenge. On April 12th, 1980, he began his "Marathon of Hope" by dipping his artificial foot into the Atlantic Ocean, with one strong leg and one prosthetic limb limping along the way, his aim was to cross the vast continent of North America coast to coast to raise twenty-four million dollars. On average, he walked about forty-eight kilometers a day. His brother, who accompanied him, was astounded by Terry's determination. Terry was in constant pain, yet he kept moving forward, propelled by his spirit of hope and faith in finding the cure for cancer. After 5,373 kilometers, halfway through his journey, the cancer spread to his lungs, cutting short his life and his goal. His spirit, however, stayed forever. Today, his heroic perseverance is commemorated through numerous awards, research grants, and an annual fund-raising run held in 60 countries in his name. His short life, filled with sacrifice, courage, and a positive attitude was an inspiration to millions. With love for others and faith in himself, he started a journey of hope. Terry Fox recreated himself, transforming a man with a fatal disease into a vision of hope for others.

Terry Fox is a great example of how, when moved by the spirit, even physical pain and suffering cannot prevent us from extraordinary achievement. Actions speak louder than words. In the Bahá'í Faith, idle talk is very much discouraged. Prayer and meditation alone are not enough to discover the true self; one must engage in action. Bahá'u'lláh gives a stern warning about lack of action in one's life with these words:

> The essence of faith is fewness of words and abundance of deeds; he whose words exceed

his deeds, know verily his death is better than his life.³

Moreover, we should not confine our deeds to helping only ourselves or immediate families. We must adopt a global consciousness. This means regarding humanity as one family. It means taking responsibility for being a member of this family. On a planet of billions of people, our good deeds can reach out to embrace people in any town, any country, any continent, wherever there is a need. This openness is another great phenomena of the age we live in.

What deeds are acceptable in the sight of God? In the following beautifully-written passage, Bahá'u'lláh tells us:

> Be generous in prosperity, and thankful in adversity. Be worthy of the trust of thy neighbor, and look upon him with a bright and friendly face. Be a treasure to the poor, an admonisher to the rich, an answerer of the cry of the needy, a preserver of the sanctity of thy pledge. Be fair in thy judgment, and guarded in

thy speech. Be unjust to no man and show all meekness to all men. Be as a lamp unto them that walk in darkness, a joy to the sorrowful, a sea for the thirsty, a haven for the distressed, an upholder and defender of the victim of oppression. Let integrity and uprightness distinguish all thine acts. Be a home for the stranger, a balm to the suffering, a tower of strength for the fugitive. Be eyes to the blind, and a guiding light unto the feet of the erring. Be an ornament to the countenance of truth, a crown to the brow of fidelity, a pillar of the temple of righteousness, a breath of life to the body of mankind, an ensign of the hosts of justice, a luminary above the horizon of virtue, a dew to the soil of the human heart, an ark on the ocean of knowledge, a sun in the heaven of bounty, a gem on the diadem of wisdom, a shining light in the firmament of thy generation, a fruit upon the tree of humility."[4]

I have read this passage many times throughout my life. At different times, different parts resonate with me. How about you?

Now let's define philanthropy. This action—an impulse generated from a deep concern for the welfare and advancement of humanity—is usually manifested by donation of money and property. To many philanthropists, it means devoting their time to activities that help the needy, the poor, and the sick. They listen to the cry of suffering whether close to home or in remote corners of the world. In their hearts, they find ways to respond.

Since the dawn of Bahá'u'lláh's revelation, this philanthropic impulse has expanded dramatically. I don't mean in the Bahá'í world only; rather, there is a movement as deep and wide as the ocean, impelling people from all parts of the globe to come forward to help their fellow humans.

Starting right at the top, consider the Bill and Melinda Gates Foundation. I knew Bill in the early 80's, not personally but as a programmer who had used some of the earliest software tools he developed. Over the next ten years, his company Microsoft grew from a start-up to a major multinational corporation. The software sold by Microsoft not only changed the computing world but transformed business and society. As the CEO and founder of Microsoft, Gates was the wealthiest man in the world from 1995 through 2011, except in 2008 when he ranked third. His worth has reached around 40 billion dollars. In 2008, Gates announced that he would be working full-time for the Bill and Melinda Gates Foundation, which he and his wife had created a few years earlier. The Foundation's achievements are impressive. Known for its financial transparency, it had spent about $28 billion on charity by 2007. It deployed funds to address global problems that have often been ignored by governments, including the fight against polio, development of agriculture to improve nutrition, providing education on the benefits of breast-feeding, and eradicating malaria. Its projects are always global in scope.

Nor is Gates alone. More and more billionaires are joining the charity club. Warren Buffet, a friend of Bill Gates and a well-admired investor in the business world, has given about $20 billion to the Bill and Melinda Gates Foundation. When asked about enlisting others to this noble cause, Buffet said, "In most cases we had reason to believe that the people already had an interest in philanthropy. It was a very soft sell but 40 have signed up." In this campaign, he was asking U.S. billionaires to give at least half of their wealth. Philanthropy has become trendy!

This spirit of charity is not restricted to business leaders, either. A number of politicians, after retiring from public service, have used their experience, knowledge and connections to help the needy. Former U.S. president Bill Clinton formed the Clinton Global Initiative, an organization community of leaders dedicated to building a sustainable world. According to its mission statement, "CGI is to inspire, connect, and empower a community of global leaders to forge solutions to the world's most pressing challenges." Its members have made nearly 2,000 commitments to action in the fields of education, health, and economy that will improve lives of 300 million people in more than 180 countries. The cost of these commitments will exceed $63 billion.

Another politician turned philanthropist is Tony Blair, former prime minister of England. His organization, the Tony Blair Faith Foundation, aims at promoting respect and understanding between major religions. He uses faith to unite diverse groups and combat extreme poverty in over 100 countries.

In 1982, former U.S. president Jimmy Carter founded a not-for-profit organization named the Carter Center. As a politician and as a philanthropist, his aim has always been to promote human rights and reduce suffering. His decades of effort towards peace in the Middle East earned him the Nobel Peace Prize. Moreover, Carter has worked to improve health around the world and is a key figure in Habitat For Humanity, a worldwide organization building affordable homes for the poor.

Hollywood stars have also jumped on the philanthropy bandwagon. Academy Award winner Angelina Jolie Voight is well known for promoting humanitarian causes. As a Goodwill Ambassador for the United Nations, she has shown great compassion for the underprivileged of the world. Through this organization, she has undertaken special missions to disaster zones including as Sierra Leon, Pakistan, Haiti, Cambodia, Tanzania and many more. "We cannot close ourselves off and ignore the fact that millions of people are out there suffering," Jolie said, "I honestly want to help. I don't believe I feel differently from other people. I think we all want justice and equality, a chance for a life with meaning. All of us would like to believe that if we were in a bad situation someone would help us." Hundreds of other celebrities are associated with organizations to fight poverty, AIDS, illiteracy and injustice. Some, like Oprah Winfrey and Jennifer Aniston, have created their own foundations, capitalizing on their wealth, power, and popularity to combat poverty, illness, abuse, and conflict.

Professional philanthropic organizations have also joined the parade. Doctors Without Borders is a well-known organization of doctors and nurses who volunteer their services in war zones and natural disaster areas. In nearly anyplace devastated by earthquake, hurricane, tsunami, drought, or and war, these professionals will be found, rendering medical services, saving lives, and staving off the catastrophic spread of disease. In 2011 alone, these medical professionals, at considerable personal risk, served in Somalia, Japan, Haiti, Yemen, the Democratic Republic of Congo, Pakistan, Bahrain, and Libya.

Philanthropy doesn't have to involve billions of dollars and a global effort. At the local level, retirees are donating their experience, time, and effort to hospitals and community services. In my own Bahá'í community of Newmarket, north of Toronto, Ontario, spearheaded by Lisa Yazdani, community members signed up to supply meals for one day at "In from the Cold," a community service for the homeless. Fifteen individuals, both adults and youth, volunteered to help. A few days before the event, the team bought enough food for 150 meals. Some showed up early in the morning to cook, and the cost of the food was funded by the Local Spiritual Assembly. At meal times, more volunteers arrived at the shelter to serve food. At the end of the day, about ninety guest showed up, one as young as 2 weeks and some in their sixties. The management was impressed with the maturity, friendliness and politeness with which the service was provided by the youth. The experience was so rewarding that the Bahá'í community volunteered to participate in more service activities in coming years.

Who says the sky is falling? Not according to the work of these noble souls! And as significant as their deeds are, they are only a small part of a global philanthropic movement that covers humanity like a comfort blanket. Individuals, organizations, and businesses around the world have found in their hearts a place for the needy. Like a deep and wide river, the spirit of service and charity flows onward, thought it may not always grab headlines. Such deeds are the very embodiment of those spiritual attributes mentioned by Bahá'u'lláh's in the quotation presented earlier. And all this work is part of God's plan to build a paradise on Earth. Everyone is part of it.

Reflection

Do you do any volunteer work? What do you think of Bahá'u'lláh's list of deeds mentioned earlier?

Deeds (path of service)

Here is another example of philanthropic deeds at grass root level.

The Baha'is of King (a town north of Toronto) have adopted and maintained a portion of the King Road that intersects with highway 400, between Weston Road and Jane Street for the last thirteen years. As a result a sign was posted by York Regional Roads acknowledging our efforts. The sign reads "Adopted by The Baha'is of York Region"

This effort was met with many challenges, especially getting volunteers to participate but many community members of King were steadfast in their service to the community. Every year the local media was informed of this project but there was no acknowledgement from the papers until ten years had passed. In the recent years, many articles were written on the local papers regarding the deeds of the Baha'is of King.

Do you have any thoughts on how locally residents can get involved in helping the larger community?

CHAPTER 6

Self-sacrifice

When we examine life in nature and a prophet's journey on this planet Earth we find they have two things in common: neither involves freewill, and sacrifice is part of their destiny. Ordinary humans have been given freewill to do whatever they want with their lives. However, for them to be admitted to true paradise, they must sacrifice their free choice to a higher order. The second barrier is suffering, which we love to avoid. To sacrifice the self, suffering is necessary and choosing to take that path is the greatest dilemma a soul faces in its awesome spiritual journey. Sacrifice, like water to a plant, is absolutely necessary for the tree of humanity to grow and flourish to the fullest.

Devotion

☼

O my brother! A pure heart is like unto a mirror; polish it with the purity of love and severance from all else save God, until the ideal sun may reflect therein, and the eternal morn may dawn. Then wilt thou find clear and manifest the meaning of: "Neither doth My earth nor My heaven occupy Me, but the heart of My faithful servant occupieth Me" -- and wilt take thy life in thy hands and sacrifice it, with a thousand longings, to the new Beloved.[1]

☼

Consider what was the fate of so many and diverse empires and peoples: the Roman Empire, France, Germany, Russia, England, etc.; all were gathered together under the same tent -- that is to say, the appearance of Christ brought about a union among these diverse nations, some of whom, under the influence of Christianity, became so united that they

☼

sacrificed their lives and property for one another.[2]

Deeper Learning

Self-sacrifice is the fifth channel through which we can receive "merciful gifts and powers". As we will see, sacrifice rejuvenates creation and sustains life on this planet, yet this sacred act is very different from other daily spiritual obligations such as prayer, reading the Holy Writings, or acquiring virtues. What is sacrifice? The dictionary definition is surrender or destruction of something prized or desirable for the sake of something considered as having a higher or more pressing claim. Throughout the ages, giving part of one's livelihood, such as a lamb or money, to a deity at an altar or shrine has been an important part of religious tradition.

When we examine nature, what we find that sacrifice plays a critical role in maintaining life on Earth. Without it, the planet would become barren as Mars. The mineral gives up its identity to become assimilated into the nature of the plant; the plant sacrifices itself for the higher existence of animals and humans. In the animal kingdom, some species prey on others for their survival. Nature sustains itself through this circle of sacrifice, giving the appearance of a hierarchy in which a lower form of existence gives up its identity for a higher form. Any change in this hierarchy can disturb the balance of nature. For example, certain birds need insects, seeds, and worms to live. If these food sources disappear, the birds that rely upon them would go extinct. All the creatures living on Earth are interconnected in complex ways through this principle of sacrifice.

In human life, sacrifice takes several forms. Offering something of value to the Divine powers can be a way of showing devotion, thankfulness, or commitment. People may make sacrifices for humanitarian purposes by donating money or time to charitable or service organizations, or they may do without things they want in order to help their children or other family members. Many consider sacrifice of time or material things as a form of worship.

So far we've considered the sacrifice of material wealth or time. But of greater import is self-sacrifice, which is a gateway to the Kingdom of God. Let's look at a few forms of this noble act.

Consider parenting. Raising a child from infancy to maturity is no easy task, requiring unconditional love as well as considerable care, courage, patience, and other virtues. Responsible parents set aside their own wishes and desires to build a strong family. Their primary hope for is the well-being of their children. They undertake this without hope for reward, financial or otherwise. Though parenting is neither glamorous nor usually highly-lauded, God considers it a meritorious act. A prosperous world civilization depends upon good parenting.

From the earliest days of the Bahá'í Faith, believers were called upon to carry the Message of their new religion throughout the world. Many loyal and obedient Bahá'ís left the security and comfort of their homes and moved to different towns, countries, and even continents. Often facing hardship—whether because jobs were scarce, climates were harsh, or cultural differences seemed overwhelming, these valiant pioneers accepted sacrifice and considered it as water to the growth of their beloved Faith.

The act of offering the self, rather than money or property, for a greater good requires wisdom, love, and faith. The ultimate example of self-sacrifice is found in the lives of the Prophets. The Biblical tale of Abraham's near-sacrifice of his son comes to mind. Many Prophets suffered persecution and even death to bring God's message to humanity. Think of the dramatic sacrifices made by Jesus and the Báb. Speaking of Christ's pain and suffering, Bahá'u'lláh said:

> Know thou that when the Son of Man yielded up His breath to God, the whole creation wept with a great weeping. By sacrificing Himself, however, a fresh capacity was infused into all created things.[3]

This is part of the Prophet's job description: "By their sanction and authority, every Prophet of God hath drunk from the chalice of sacrifice…"[4] They willingly make these sacrifices to achieve the greatest good imaginable: leading us to God.

On the June 23rd, 1870, Mírzá Mihdí, Bahá'u'lláh's youngest son, while walking on a rooftop engrossed in thoughtful prayer, accidentally fell through a skylight and was critically injured. Bahá'u'lláh offered to heal him but Mírzá Mihdí requested instead that "his life be accepted as a ransom for those who were prevented from attaining the presence of their Beloved."[5] Bahá'u'lláh accepted His son's wish; Mírzá Mihdí died at the age of twenty-two.

The ultimate goal for any soul should be to sacrifice for God. Most of us will not be called to such a dramatic sacrifice as Christ's crucifixion; rather ours will be a slow, conscious effort towards giving up self for the sake of the Creator.

But why would anyone want to do so? Detachment from self is hard work! Let's ponder this by looking at a few significant examples. In the animal kingdom, sacrifice is compelled. Does the fly really want to be food for the birds? Does a deer want to be dinner for a wolf? No. They do not make sacrifices consciously, yet their sacrifices are essential to the cycle of life.

For humans, however, the act of self-sacrifice can only happen as a conscious decision. And indeed, there are any number of brilliant examples of this throughout history.

Consider Nelson Mandela, who championed freedom during the apartheid regime of South Africa.

Apartheid was a system of legal segregation imposed by the ruling government of South Africa between 1948 and 1994. Under this regime, the rights of the majority 'non-white' population were reduced in favor of the white minority. The government enforced racial separation in education, medical care, and public spaces such as beaches. Black people routinely received inferior service compared to their white citizens. In December 1956, when Mandela and others protested against this injustice in their native land, they were arrested and imprisoned. Later, Mandela was tried as the leader of the ANC and was found guilty.

As part of his closing statement at his trial, Mandela said: "During my lifetime I have dedicated myself to the struggle of the African people. I have fought against white domination, and I have fought against black domination. I have cherished the ideal of a democratic and free society in which all persons live together in harmony and with equal opportunities. It is an ideal which I hope to live for and to achieve. But if needs be, it is an ideal for which I am prepared to die."

Mandela was sentenced to life imprisonment. He was thrown in the D-group prison with the lowest privileges, with one letter and one visitor every six month. After 27 years in confinement, Mandela was released in 1990, an event widely applauded throughout the world. In 1994 apartheid in Africa came to an end.

Though long in captivity, Mandela's spirit was always free. He obtained a law degree from University of London. He corresponded with world leaders to fight for the cause of freedom, human dignity, and justice. After gaining his freedom, he became the President of South Africa and was true to his words. He held no bitterness toward white South Africans and treated people of all races with respect and justice, something he was denied of over most of his life.

Racial segregation was also a fact of life across the Atlantic Ocean in the southern states of America. It was a common public transportation practice, for example, to require black people to sit in the back of the bus, reserving the forward seating for white people. When a bus was full, black passengers boarding were required to stand. If a white person boarded the bus, everyone in the black row nearest the front had to get up and stand, so that a new row for white passengers could be created.

In December, 1955, Rosa Park, an African-American, boarded the bus and took a seat in the foremost row reserved for black riders. After a few stops, the seats for Caucasians filled up. When another white man boarded the bus, the driver asked everyone in Park's row to move to the back to make room for the whites. Everyone complied except Park. Her refusal earned Park an arrest and, upon being found guilty, a $10 fine plus an additional $4 for court costs. Some consider this incident to be the start of the American Civil Rights Movement. Martin Luther King, who became the most iconic figures of this movement, was assassinated on April 4, 1968. Like him, thousands, both white and black, joined the fight against social injustice. Without going into too much detail of this movement, three points are clear.

1. Participants in this movement made a clear choice that put their lives at risk.
2. During this turbulent time in America, thousands were jailed, homes and other properties were burned to the ground, many

were beaten and tortured, and some were killed.
3. These sacrifices led directly to changes in the law that prohibited segregation and sought to prevent or redress other forms of racial discrimination.

Decades before the ordeals of Mandela and King, their hero Mahatma Gandhi employed nonviolent means to fight the oppression arising from the British Empire's colonization of India. He was put in jail for his protest. Eventually Gandhi's aim was realized when India gained independence, but he paid the ultimate price when he was assassinated.

History is filled with stories of heroic deeds that have completely changed the direction of human lives. Like Gandhi, Mandela, Park, and King, countless others have fought for equality, justice, and peace over decades and centuries. In 2011, during the Arab Spring, thousands sacrificed their lives in Egypt, Libya, Yemen, and Syria. Ordinary citizens, yearning for freedom from tyranny, faced the mighty armies of their oppressors and knowingly put themselves in the path of danger. It was a price they were willing to pay.

One brave women, Tawakkul Karman almost single-handedly launched Yemen's protest movement. In a society where women walked behind their husbands, she was a long-time activist who had been warned many times that she was putting her life at risk. Yet she was as undeterred as her heroes: Martin Luther King, Nelson Mandela, and Mahatma Gandhi, pictures of whom hung on the wall of her radio studio/sitting room. Karman won the 2011 Nobel Peace Prize. This prize was shared with two other women, Ellen Johnson Sirleaf and Leymah Gbowee, both of whom had fought for peace and women's rights in Liberia.

This glimpse at the power of self-sacrifice shows that through it societies are lifted to a higher level. It seems there is a mystical connection between sacrifice and progress: when blood and tears are shed, the Holy Spirit seems to shower bounties in abundance upon humanity. Through sacrifice, we realize our collective potential and are led onward toward the Most Great Peace.

Self-sacrifice means action. Progress does not come from prayer and meditation alone. Nor is knowledge enough. We can read every book in the world and gain as much knowledge as we like, but until that knowledge is put into action, it does no good. When we arise to action, the Holy Spirit comes to our assistance to provide us all we need to make ourselves and our societies better. Our powers of courage, love, patience, and words are increased. Just think of the power of the great teachers, pioneers, and martyrs and how they helped advance the Cause of God. Reflect on those who gave up their lives to promote equality, justice, health, literacy, or any other cause of significance.

Ultimately, the greatest form of self-sacrifice is that undertaken for God. 'Abdu'l-Bahá explains it this way:

> O illustrious Ismael! All the friends of God should be as a sacrifice unto the One true God. This means that they should sacrifice and immolate all that pertaineth to them for the Beauty of God so that in this way they may reach the state of annihilation in God, which is none other than being a total sacrifice in His

Lordship. This entails renouncing one's own wishes, one's own good pleasure, and desire and servitude to the servants of the Abhá Beauty, may my life be a ransom unto His loved ones![6]

When I reflect on this passage, one thing becomes clear: through total surrender of the self, by sacrificing free will to abide by the Will of God, we are led to our goal: the "blissful abode of the Divine Presence." When collectively we sacrifice our will to God's Will, gradually we see the Kingdom of God being constructed in front of our eyes.

There is a paradox in sacrifice. Giving often means pain, which our animal side instinctively avoids. Yet there is a sweet taste to this bitter experience. A four year-old boy, Jason Mackintosh, was diagnosed with bone cancer and had only six months to live. His parents were determined to find a cure for his illness at any cost. Eventually they lost their home, accumulated a mountain of debt, the mother had to quit her job, and both parents agonized over their son's destiny, but they never gave up. When Jason passed away after 11 months, the mother said, "For Jason, we would do it all over again." She wiped tears rolling down the cheek. "Maybe more. A million times over." For the love of their child, the sacrifice of these parents knew no bounds. I think the same is true of anyone who has given up the self for any higher cause. If done for God, the taste of sacrifice is even sweeter.

Reflection

When you think of self-sacrifice, what emotional response do you have?

After reading this presentation, did your understanding of sacrifice change?

What powers and gifts are obtained through sacrifice?

Deeds (path of service)

I mediated on philanthropic deeds and self-sacrifice. Both go hand in hand; both contribute tremendously to reshaping us, individually and collectively, and both are manifestations of caring for others. I concluded that each is powered by different attributes. Philanthropy is driven by altruism and compassion. When we choose self-sacrifice, do we do it out of love (parenting) or to combat injustice (Gandhi)? What do you think?

CHAPTER 7

Severance from this world

Severance from this world is not easy. Many with spiritual beliefs are certain of why we are on this planet and where we go after we die. They believe the body releases the soul, which then takes flight to its natural existence. What happens to this being thereafter depends on what it does here according to many Holy Scriptures, such as the Bible, Qur'án, Bhagavad Gita and Bahá'í Writings. There are many hurdles to overcome in this world, all of which will benefit us in the next one. Identifying those hurdles and overcoming them is the key to spiritual success.

Devotion

☼

O My Brother! A pure heart is as a mirror; cleanse it with the burnish of love and severance from all save God, that the true sun may shine within it and the eternal morning dawn. Then wilt thou clearly see the meaning of "Neither doth My earth nor My heaven contain Me, but the heart of My faithful servant containeth Me." And thou wilt take up thy life in thine hand, and with infinite longing cast it before the new Beloved One.[1]

☼

These are the mysteries of the words which are clearly unfolded and unveiled that thou mayest comprehend the morn of significances and extinguish the lamp of superstition, fancy, doubt and suspicion through the power of reliance and severance, and light the new lamp of knowledge and assurance in the recess of mind and heart.[2]

☼

Deeper Learning

What is severance? It means to be detached, disengaged, and to have no emotional involvement. How can we live without any engagement in everyday activities such as study, work, teaching, or eating? Without enthusiasm, it is hard to be successful in whatever tasks we undertake. If God created this planet and put us here to live out a part of our existence, why would He ask us to be detached from this world? This sounds confusing and contradictory.

'Abdu'l-Bahá gives us a precise definition of detachment. He said:

> Detachment does not consist in setting fire to one's house, or becoming bankrupt or throwing one's fortune out of the window, or even giving away all of one's possessions. Detachment consists in refraining from letting our possessions possess us.[3]

The Master is warning us that this world is full of distractions. Our spiritual development is so important that it will not only affect our lives here but also in the hereafter. As in any important endeavor, in order to achieve a cherished goal, the mind must maintain a laser-like focus. This is doubly true for our spiritual aspirations. If we do not keep the target in mind, less important matters can easily derail lives.

To better understand these distractions, let's consider a hypothetical example: Scott O'Neil got straight A's at Pearson High School. Very popular among his peers, he was elected president of Student Council for two consecutive years and was later admitted to the Princeton Engineering School with a scholarship. With his parents' hearts overflowing with pride, Scott left his home in rural Wisconsin, confident that he would make his loved ones and admirers even more proud. He settled into campus life and quickly made several friends. Scott quickly recognized that he had something new in his life: a freedom he had never felt before. With no parents to watch over him and supervise, he could study whenever he wanted to and do whatever he wanted. In fact, Scott did very little studying and spent most of his time with his new girlfriend and hanging out at the local bar (resulting in many hangovers). Scott also started experimenting with drugs. He always told himself, "I can change any time I want." He started missing assignment deadlines, which he rationalized by telling himself, "I know I can catch up." But he couldn't. In fact, he ended the school year with an embarrassingly average C+, a grade far below his capabilities. He lost his scholarship and was forced to return home to take up work at his uncle's butcher shop.

This story is fiction, but similar stories play out in real life all the time.

- Detachment is often misunderstood. It does not mean that:
- You don't care about anything
- You do not take responsibility for anything
- You do not participate in anything
- You ignore the needs and feelings of others

According to Bahá'u'lláh, this world and all it contains is meant for us to enjoy. At the same time, the soul has been given a sacred responsibility to approach its Creator by developing spiritual qualities. The "world" from which we must become detached consists of those things that cause us to forget the real purpose of life. After all, no one lives on this plane forever. Sooner or later we are all compelled to leave it, and once we enter the next realm, we will become fully aware of our spiritual condition and of what our life here accomplished. It can be a scary thought. As we have seen before, we need to achieve a balance by walking the physical path with an eye on heaven.

How do we know when the balance has tipped too much towards the things of this world? I think emotion is a good barometer. Let's look at three examples:

A man becomes so obsessed with gambling that he loses time and money on it every week while neglecting the needs of his family.

Scott's goal of getting a good education at Princeton was (in the story told above) replaced by the enjoyment of doing whatever he felt like doing, which led to reckless behavior.

The very real Darius I was a much-liked king of ancient Persia. Unlike his predecessors, his popularity grew because of his spiritual qualities. He fashioned a society based on justice, kindness, and generosity. Darius was fascinated by, perhaps even secretly envied, the lifestyle of the dervish. Dervishes were known for renouncing the material world and roaming the countryside, spending every waking moment in devotion and praise of God. A dervish's possessions usually included only his clothes and a basket in which to carry a few small belongings often given to him by well-wishers. Darius was so attracted to this simple spiritual lifestyle that he invited a well-known dervish to his palace.

When the dervish arrived, the king sat at his feet and requested that he expound upon detachment. The dervish was delighted by the king's interest. He stayed in Darius' palace for a few days and, whenever the king had time, the dervish would teach him about the virtues of a mendicant's life. On the third day, after careful consideration of all he had learned thus far, the king decided to leave the palace, his family, and all the comforts known to him in order that he might join the dervish.

The next day, dressed in the garb of a poor man, the king left behind his worldly possessions and walked in the company of the dervish. By dusk they had already traveled far. When it came time for them to retire for the night, the dervish realized he had left his basket at the palace. Looking very disturbed he said, "I beg you, we have to go back to get my basket!" The king replied, "We can manage without the basket. Some generous soul will give us one." The dervish looked very determined, and exclaimed, "I cannot continue without the basket!" Shocked by the attitude and behavior of the dervish, the king exclaimed, "I, a king, have abandoned my palace, wealth, and power. You, who preach the virtues of detachment, have been tested by this virtue and failed because you are attached to this world—to a small basket."

Based on my experience and the accounts of others, it seems to me there is a relationship between how a prayer is answered and the emotional detachment of the supplicant from specific expectations of divine help. For example, I have had prayers answered only long after I made the plea. It seems I never get my prayers answered right away. Once I waited forty years for an answer, and by then I did not care if I got what I had asked God for. Suddenly doors opened up, things fell into place, and the prayer was answered. Do you find you must become detached before your prayers are answered?

Besides emotional distractions and attachments, there are at least three other obstacles we must avoid if we are to achieve the purpose of life, to "know and worship God." These traps are materialism, imitation, and self-glorification.

To illustrate materialism, consider the fictional case of Steve Kalichuck, a very successful cosmetic surgeon who has one simple goal: to enjoy life as possible. For Steve, there is no life beyond death. Therefore, he must make the most of this life, which to him means to enjoy it as much as possible. He adorns himself with gold jewelry, wears expensive designer clothing, lives in a luxurious home, takes exotic vacations, and drives fast cars. His wife and three children share his values. When they do not get what they want, they become angry, jealous, and are often rude towards others and even each other. Focused as they are on the material, they miss opportunities to develop spiritual qualities. This family has not experienced its spiritual birth.

Now consider imitation, which can be characterized as an attachment to archaic ideas, distorted visions, outworn traditions, and counterproductive habits. All such attachments are veils blocking our spiritual vision.

Bahá'u'lláh taught that periodically a new Messenger from God comes with fresh teachings. When that happens, only few accept the new revelation. For example, at the time of Christ's death, only few accepted His teachings because He did not fulfill their expectations for the Messiah. Likewise, today traditions regarding the second coming of Christ bar many from considering that the expected event may already have happened. These barriers are reinforced by the fact that most people follow the religion of their parents. Finally, we come to self-glorification, which can be viewed as an attachment to one's own virtues, whether real or perceived. Intelligence is a virtue but we can become arrogant if we dwell too much on this quality. Having intelligence only benefits us if we practice humility. Virtues naturally become part of our identity and can be seen in our spiritual accomplishments. However, a divine quality can also become a hurdle when we become self-righteous. When we start to feel superior to others, our arrogance will be manifested in our behavior. For example, a kind person who grows proud of his kindness may start to perform "acts of kindness" not to be kind but to show off. He may further start to judge others as less kind than himself. The resulting behavior will be anything but kind. Pride and the tendency to view others as inferior is a sure sign of attachment to divine qualities. Spiritual maturity, on the other hand, is evidenced by the ability to recognize that every soul has received its fair share of divine grace. We must cultivate humility to the same degree that we do other divine qualities.

This attachment is the most dangerous of all. It is like the arrow that shoots down a high-flying bird. No matter how advanced, a soul can be brought crashing to the ground if wounded by the arrows of jealousy, lust, power, greed, or self-adoration. Everything around us from food and clothing to family and friendship has been created for our enjoyment. When gained in legitimate ways, we should enjoy them wholeheartedly and be truly thankful for them. None of these things, however, should ever become like gods to us, overshadowing our true God and causing us to forget Him. None of them should eclipse the light of the Holy Spirit; none of them should extinguish the spirit of faith from our hearts. We must always be vigilant lest any attachment distract us from our real purpose.

A balanced life grows our spiritual powers and expands our awareness beyond imagination. Rarely do we recognize the wonders surrounding us and of which we are a part. Let the Lord of this Day explain:

> O my brother, understand then the meaning of resurrection and purify thine ears from the saying of these rejected people. Shouldst thou step a little way into the worlds of severance, thou wilt testify that no day greater than this Day and no resurrection mightier than this Resurrection can be imagined, and that one deed in this Day is equivalent to deeds performed during a hundred thousand years -- nay, I ask pardon of God for this limitation, because deeds done in this Day are sanctified beyond any limited reward.[4]

The proof of the greatness of this age surrounds us, but a discerning eye is required to recognize it. If we focus on the stories told by the news media, mostly we will hear the negative: financial crises, natural disasters, crime, armed rebellion. Such events are an aspect of this age, forcing us to seek better solutions to our problems, but they are not the whole story. Wonderful things, too, happen all the time all around the world.

For example, international cooperation is increasing on many fronts such as the G20, a group of finance ministers and central bank governors from nineteen countries plus the European Union who have met periodically since 2008 to discuss global economic policies. Humanity faces a great many challenges—not only economic ones—as a truly global civilization evolves, but international efforts are being made on many fronts to address them.

Reflection

We focused on distractions, emotional detachment, materialism, imitation, and self-glorification as obstacles spiritual progress. Are there any others?

What divine gifts and powers are to be obtained through detachment?

Deeds (path of service)

While good deeds are praiseworthy, the motives behind them are also important. Are they done for self-satisfaction? To benefit of society? For the sake of God?

CHAPTER 8

Sanctity

In every religion, sanctity or purity is the goal of the believer. The meaning and purpose of sanctity are some of religion's most commonly misunderstood concepts. The ideas are very simple, yet achieving holiness through sanctity is the believer's most challenging task.

Devotion

☼

> We entreat Our loved ones not to besmirch the hem of Our raiment with the dust of falsehood, neither to allow references to what they have regarded as miracles and prodigies to debase Our rank and station, or to mar the purity and sanctity of Our name.[1]

☼

Should there be ignited in thy heart the burning brand of the love of God, thou wouldst seek neither rest nor composure, neither laughter nor repose, but wouldst hasten to scale the highest summits in the realms of divine nearness, sanctity, and beauty.[2]

Deeper Learning

What is sanctity? When applied to humanity it means holiness, saintliness, or godliness. It may also refer to the character of a special place such as a temple, which is considered to be sacred or hallowed in character. Sanctity can be thought of as a ladder on which the higher one climbs, the self is emptied of worldly desire and filled with God's love. With each rung ascended, the process of purification advances.

We use water for physical cleansing, but in many religions, it is a symbol of spiritual purification. During baptism, Protestants sprinkle or immerse themselves in water. Hindus take a bath in the holy water of the Ganges River, a symbolic act of cleansing the inner self. Islam elevates cleanliness to a high standard, and introduces ablutions, the ritual washing of hands and face and the wiping of the head before prayer. According to Quranic law, this is performed five times a day. Other laws relate to physical purification such as bathing, the wearing of scents, the cleaning of cloth, the usage of brushes, avoidance of spitting, and the introduction of handkerchiefs. The same "immaculate cleanliness" was commanded by the Báb and Bahá'u'lláh. Based on their instructions, Bahá'ís around the world practice the following:

> Before prayer the hands and face are to be washed. If there is no water, it is sufficient to speak the verse: "*Bismi'lláh al-athar al-athar.*" (In the Name of God, the Most Pure, the Most Pure)

Associating with people of other religions is not considered impure.

Bahá'ís are instructed to wash their feet every day in summer, and every third day during winter time.

The renewal of one's household effects every nineteen years.

The scriptures of the Bahá'í Faith have a lot to say on various aspects of sanctity. For example, in the "Table of Purity," 'Abdu'l-Bahá, clearly identifies sanctity with purity and defines it as an essential characteristic for a soul to acquire on the road to perfection. He says:

> Cleanliness and sanctity in all conditions are characteristics of pure beings and necessities of free souls. The first perfection consists in cleanliness and sanctity and in purity from every defect. When man in all conditions is pure and immaculate, he will become the center of the reflection of the manifest Light. In all his actions and conduct there must first be purity, then beauty and independence.[3]

In this Tablet, the Master dwells on physical cleanliness as a starting point for overall purity. He adds:

> ...although bodily cleanliness is a physical thing, it hath, nevertheless, a powerful

influence on the life of the spirit. It is even as a voice wondrously sweet, or a melody played...

Cleanliness is important for physical health and to prevent the spread of disease. Yet we also have to exercise balance. Some researchers think that excessive cleanliness may be partly responsible for the rise in allergies!

The "Tablet of Purity" also warns us about what we put into our bodies. Tobacco, alcohol, and opiates are all harmful and to be avoided. They not only take a toll on our bodies, but their spiritual effects are subtle and long-lasting. Likewise, proper nutrition requires attention. Consider the body to be the temple of the soul and it becomes obvious that it should be respected and well-cared for.

As important as it may be, physical purity is only the beginning. Consider the Sermon on the Mount is considered the greatest address Jesus Christ gave to His followers. Sitting on a mountain near Capernaum, He delivered the Word of God, providing beatitudes, new laws, and the Lord's Prayer. Among other things, He spoke these words: 'Happy are the pure in heart; they will see God!"[4] In this divine counsel, three elements are connected: happiness, purity, and closeness to God.

Purity has the power to lift us up to a blissful existence. In Buddhism, it is closely related to Nirvana, the ultimate goal of every Buddhist. The last of the Buddha's Four Noble Truths is that to reach the highest plateau of peace, we must break away from the cycle of suffering. In His own words: "Free from impurities, I did attain unto the utter Peace of Nirvana."[5] Gold is purified through searing heat; for the soul, according to Buddha, that heat is suffering. Similarly, the Hindu Avatar Krishna said: "Freedom from fear, purity of heart .... these are the qualities of the man who is born for heaven."[6] In Islam, it is said that paradise consisting of "Gardens of Eden, beneath whose trees the rivers flow" will be the "reward of him who hath been pure."[7] God gave Moses the task of bringing Pharaoh a message from God: "Hast thou the will to purify thyself, and that I should guide thee to thy Lord, then thou shalt fear?"[8]

In the same vein, the Báb revealed in the Persian Bayán: "God loveth those who are pure."[9] Bahá'u'lláh wrote, "Every pure, every refined and sanctified soul will be endowed with tremendous power, and shall rejoice with exceeding gladness"[10] From these passages, it is obvious that if our goal is true happiness, which is the same as being close to God, purity of heart is essential.

Who does not want to experience happiness, tranquility, paradise, Nirvana and peace? Given that religion offers a clear path to this goal, why would so many people be fleeing from religion? Part of the answer may be that religion's prescription is harder to swallow than the alternatives offered by the material world. Happiness of a sort can be found in food, drink, games, and other entertainments. In a stressful world, these are sold alongside other practices such as yoga, tai-chi and meditative exercises as means to happiness.

But the happiness brought by such means is often short-lived. The happiness promised by religion is deeper and more permanent, but attaining to it is much harder than paying for entertainment. Religion makes us look deep into our souls and calls us to cleanse ourselves of whatever impurities we find there until we reflect the most glorious divine attributes. And this is painful. But hard as it may be, the path to the Divine Presence is open to all regardless of creed or nationality or color. All that is required is a willingness to make an effort, and God will assist. This is the promise.

Now if we need to be purified, from what must we be purified? Vice? Impure thoughts? Malicious intent? Actually, it's what underlies all such failures: the ego-self that is attached to all that belongs to this world. Purification and detachment thus go hand-in-hand. Bahá'u'lláh puts it this way:

> A pure heart is as a mirror; cleanse it with the burnish of love and severence from all save God, that the true sun may shine within it and the eternal morning dawn.[11]

According to 'Abdu'l-Bahá, purification means the purgation of the self. During His travels in America, on May 26, 1912, speaking at Mount Morris Baptist Church, He started His talk based on the hymn "Nearer my God to Thee," which He had just heard. Prompted by this song, He touched upon the meaning of cleansing the soul. He listed the many steps involved in this process, including devotion, unity, service and perfection then summarized: "In a word, nearness to God necessitates sacrifice of self, severance and the giving up of all to Him. Nearness is likeness."[12]

Though each of us is created in the image and likeness of God, not everyone reflects His beauty. The ego-self eclipses the soul, hiding its beauty. Given the true worth of a human being, Bahá'u'lláh tells us, in *The Hidden Words* and elsewhere, how to make that inherent gem "resplendent and manifest": we must "come forth from the sheath of self and desire". It is important to note that He said "self *and* desire," and not just "desire".

Suppose you could take all of your possessions—your knowledge, accomplishments, friends, daughters, sons, spouse or fiancée, accolades, emotions, skills, and material wealth—and placed them on a platter. Imagine carrying this platter to the Threshold of Bahá'u'lláh and placing it before Him. Upon sacrificing all you have in this way, you go outside, empty-handed, standing in beautiful surroundings, awaiting God's pleasure. Your heart filled with the love and knowledge of God, from then on you hear through His ears and see through His eyes, because God becomes your guide. Your soul is created anew, freed from impurities, completely aligned with the Will of God. This is nearness to God, also called Nirvana and paradise. In such a state, all you will see is God's beauty reflected in all things.

People do not usually manage such a sacrifice all at once, of course. In the path towards the "blissful abode," normally the traveler only gradually sacrifices self and desire and replenishes the emptiness with God's blessings. Purification is a difficult process, requiring great love, knowledge, detachment, and the cleansing power of suffering. Each time you succeed in placing a bit of yourself on the sacrificial altar, you take one step closer to God.

Let's look at an example. A loved one is very sick. In spite of medical attention, his health continues to deteriorate. You have expended enormous time and energy in prayer, care, and even fund-raising to help him until finally you tell yourself, "I can't do any more." It has become clear his life is ebbing, and your distress at losing him twists and turns inside you like a whirlwind. But you know you can't change the outcome, so although you love him very much, you let go, leaving the matter to God. In doing so, you have conquered yourself and by travelling the path of detachment.

The purpose of purification is to prepare for God's "descent" as mentioned in several passages in *The Hidden Words* and other passages, such as this one:

> All that is in heaven and earth I have ordained for thee, except the human heart, which I have made the habitation of My beauty and glory.[13]

Purification also has a collective aspect. When Bahá'u'lláh declared Himself to be the Promised One of all ages on April 21, 1863, the whole of creation was infused with a marvelous capacity for purification. On that Day in the Ridvan Garden, now celebrated annually as the "Most Great Festival", He said that

> ...all created things were immersed in the sea of purification. When, on that first day of Ridván, We shed upon the whole of creation the splendours of Our most excellent Names and Our most exalted Attributes.[14]

This cosmic "house cleaning" clears away centuries of accumulated error and attachment each time a new

Revelation is delivered through the Holy Spirit, preparing the way for the renew and reconstruction humanity. Such a deep cleansing is needed for both individuals and nations, so that our hearts will be made new again and our souls will be sanctified for God's "descent."

Perfection is dependent upon purity, which means seeing with the eyes of God and hearing with the ears of God. It means learning over time to do God's will. It means giving up the self and letting the Will of God work through the soul. It means being poor in self but rich in God.

> O my brother! A pure heart is like unto a mirror; polish it with the purity of love and severance from all else save God, until the ideal sun may reflect therein, and the eternal morn may dawn. Then wilt thou find clear and manifest the meaning of: "Neither doth My earth nor My heaven occupy Me, but the heart of My faithful servant occupieth Me"--and wilt take thy life in thy hands and sacrifice it, with a thousand longings, to the new Beloved.[15]

Sanctity is more than physical cleanliness, healthful living, or even purity of thought, although these are important aspects of our spiritual journey. Ultimately, sanctity is making the heart the throne of God. This is the sacred goal of the soul in its eternal journey.

Reflection

Physical cleanliness has a positive effect on us. After I take a shower, wear clean clothing or tidy up a room, I feel much better. Once I had a car and every time it was washed, it seemed to run better. Maybe it was my imagination. What is your experience when it comes to cleanliness? Does spiritual cleanliness have a similar effect? Can you make a list of powers that one can obtain through purification of the soul?

Deeds (path of service)

Knowledge, love, and faith are some of the inner powers that move us to action. Even so, walking the spiritual path is often difficult. Many obstacles, some caused by ourselves and others divinely ordained, await us along this journey. My hope in writing this book is to help strengthen your knowledge, love, and faith so as to encourage you as you walk the path to a divine life. We have a symbiotic relationship with our environment, including with each other. By helping ourselves we influence our family, neighbors, nations, and world. Moreover, loving and caring for others creates a richer environment for one's own self.

We live in a very special time in the history of mankind, a day in which gifts and powers are raining down from the realm above in abundance. Anyone can take their share of these divine bounties if one makes an effort.

Appendix A

http://www.bahai.org/ - Official international website for the Bahá'í of the world.

https://www.bic.org/ - Bahá'í International Community – United Nation Office

http://www.bahai.com/ - Information about the Bahá'í Religion

http://www.sacred-texts.com/ - Holy Writings of the Bahá'í Religion

Bibliography

Abdu'l-Baha, *Selections from the Writings of Abdu'l-Baha*, Baha'i World Centre: Haifa, 1978

'Abdu'l-Bahá, *Some Answered Questions*, US Bahá'í Publishing Trust, 1990 reprint of pocket-size edition

'Abdu'l-Bahá, *Foundations of World Unity*, US Bahá'í Publishing Trust, 1979 sixth printing

'Abdu'l-Bahá, *The Promulgation of Universal Peace,* US Bahá'í Publishing Trust, 1982 second edition

'Abdu'l-Bahá, *'Abdu'l-Bahá in London,* UK Bahá'í Publishing Trust, 1982 reprint

Bahá'í Scriptures: Selections from the Utterances of Bahá'u'lláh and 'Abdu'l-Bahá by Bahá'u'lláh and Abdu'l-Bahá, edited by Horace Holley. Bahá'í World Center, 1923

The Bab, *Selections from the Writings of the Bab*, Bahá'í World Centre, 1982 lightweight edition

Bahá'u'lláh, *The Hidden Words*, Arabic version, US Bahá'í Publishing Trust, 1985 reprint

Bahá'u'lláh, *Bahá'í Prayers,* US Bahá'í Publishing Trust, 1991 edition

Bahá'u'lláh, *Gleanings from the Writings of Bahá'u'lláh* US Bahá'í Publishing Trust, 1990 pocket-size edition

Bahá'u'lláh, *Gems of Divine Mysteries,* Haifa, Israel, Bahá'í World Centre, 2002 edition

H.M. Balyuzi, *Bahá'u'lláh - The King of Glory,* UK, George Ronald Pub Ltd (April 30, 1991)

Bhagavad Gita, Edwin Arnold translations, Dover Publications; Reprint edition (October 12, 1993)

King James Bible, Oxford University Press; 400th anniversary ed edition (Nov. 26 2010)

The Qur'an (Rodwell translation), Kessinger Publishing (Jan. 29 2010)

Deuterocanonical Apocrypha, *Wisdom,* Walter de Gruyter (Sept. 16 2011)

Reference

Full details of authors and titles are given in the bibliography.

Introduction

1. 'Abdu'l-Bahá, *Selections from the Writings of Abdu'l-Baha*, p. 203
2. 'Abdu'l-Bahá, *Foundations of World Unity*, p. 63
3. Bahá'u'lláh, *The Hidden Words*, Arabic version, no. 31

CHAPTER 1: Spiritual Birth

1. Bahá'u'lláh, *Bahá'í Prayers*, p. 16
2. Bahá'u'lláh, *Bahá'í Prayers*, p. 18
3. *King James Bible*, John, 3.3
4. *King James Bible*, John, 3.6
5. 'Abdu'l-Bahá, *The Promulgation of Universal Peace*, p. 226
6. *The Qur'an* (Rodwell tr), Sura 29 - The Spider

7 Bahá'u'lláh, *Gleanings from the Writings of Bahá'u'lláh*, p. 316

8 'Abdu'l-Bahá, *Some Answered Questions*, p.223

9 Bahá'u'lláh, *The Hidden Words*, Persian version, no. 5

CHAPTER 2: Knowledge of God

1. Bahá'u'lláh, *Epistle to the Son of the Wolf*, p. 12
2. Bahá'u'lláh, *Epistle to the Son of the Wolf*, p. 32
3. Bahá'u'lláh, *Gleanings From the Writings of Bahá'u'lláh*, p. 261
4. Baha'u'llah, *Prayers and Meditations by Baha'u'llah*, p. 313
5. Baha'u'llah, *Gleanings from the Writings of Baha'u'llah*, p. 194
6. Baha'u'llah, *Hidden Words*, Arabic version, no. 59
7. Deuterocanonical Apocrypha, *Wisdom*, no 23
8. Bible (King James version), *Genesis*, 1:26
9. 'Abdu'l-Bahá, *Paris Talks*, p. 89
10. Baha'u'llah, *Gleanings from the Writings of Baha'u'llah*, p. 49
11. Bible (King James version), *John*, 1:5
12. 'Abdu'l-Bahá, *'Abdu'l-Bahá in London*, p. 19

13. Bahá'u'lláh, *Gleanings from the Writings of Bahá'u'lláh*, p. 186
14. Bahá'u'lláh, *Gems of Divine Mysteries*, p. 42
15. 'Abdu'l-Bahá, *'Abdu'l-Bahá in London*, p. 108)

CHAPTER 3: Love of God

1. Bahá'u'lláh, *Epistle to the Son of the Wolf*, p. 13
2. Bible (King James version), Corinthians 2:9
3. Bible (King James Bible), John 4:8
4. Buddha, *The Word*, The Eightfold Path
5. Kesuvim, *Tehillim,* Psalms 40,17
6. Bible (King James version), John 4:12
7 *Qur'án*, Sura 2, "The Heifer"; translated by E. H. Palmer
8. 'Abdu'l-Bahá, *Paris Talks*, p. 179
9. 'Abdu'l-Bahá, *Paris Talks*, p. 179
10. 'Abdu'l-Bahá, *A Traveller's Narrative*, p. 4
11. 'Abdu'l-Bahá, *The Promulgation of Universal Peace*, p. 15
12. Bahá'u'lláh, *Epistle to the Son of the Wolf*, p. 26
13. Bahá'u'lláh, *Epistle to the Son of the Wolf*, p. 27

CHAPTER 4: Spirit of Faith

1. Bahá'u'lláh, *Epistle to the Son of the Wolf*, p. 13
2. Bahá'u'lláh, *Epistle to the Son of the Wolf*, p. 29
3. 'Abdu'l-Bahá, *Paris Talks*, p. 201
4. 'Abdu'l-Bahá, *The Promulgation of Universal Peace*, p. 337
5. Bahá'u'lláh, *Gleanings from the Writings of Bahá'u'lláh*, p. 143
6. Adib Taherzadeh, *The Revelation of Bahá'u'lláh*, v 4, p. 217
7. Abdu'l-Baha, *Tablets of Abdu'l-Baha*, p. 442
8. The Qur'an, (Yusuf Ali translation), Surah 40
9. H.M. Balyuzi, *Bahá'u'lláh - The King of Glory*, p. 171
10. Bahá'u'lláh, *Epistle to the Son of the Wolf*, p. 115
11. Bahá'u'lláh, *Epistle to the Son of the Wolf*, p. 135
12. Bahá'u'lláh, *Epistle to the Son of the Wolf*, p. 135

CHAPTER 5: Philanthropic Deeds

1. Bahá'u'lláh, *The Hidden Words*, Persian version, no. 5
2. Bahá'u'lláh, *Epistle to the Son of the Wolf*, p. 24
3. Bahá'u'lláh, *Epistle to the Son of the Wolf*, p. 24
4. Bahá'u'lláh, *Epistle to the Son of the Wolf*, p. 93

CHAPTER 6: Self-sacrifice

1. 'Abdu'l-Bahá, *Bahá'í Scriptures*, p. 164
2. 'Abdu'l-Bahá, *Some Answered Questions*, p. 10
3. Bahá'u'lláh, *Gleanings from the Writings of Bahá'u'lláh*, XXXVI, p. 85
4. Bahá'u'lláh, *Kitab-i-Iqan*, p. 15
5. Shoghi Effendi, *God Passes By*, p. 188
6. 'Abdu'l-Bahá, *Tablet to Ismael*

CHAPTER 7: Severance from this world

1. Bahá'u'lláh, *The Seven Valleys*, p. 21 – 22
2. Bahá'u'lláh, Bahá'í Scriptures, p. 16
3. 'Abdu'l-Bahá, *Divine Philosophy*, p. 135
4. Bahá'u'lláh, *Bahá'í Scriptures*, p. 38

CHAPTER 8: Sanctity

1. Bahá'u'lláh, *Epistle to the Son of the Wolf*, p. 33
2. Bahá'u'lláh, *Gems of Divine Mysteries*, p. 14
3. 'Abdu'l-Bahá, *Table of Purity*
4. Bible (King James version), Matthew 5:8
5. The Buddha, *Majjhima-Nikaya*, i, 160
6. *Bhagavad Gita*, 16:1-3

7. *The Qur'an* (Rodwell translation), Sura 20 - Ta. Ha

8. *The Qur'an,* (Rodwell translation), Sura 79

9. The Bab, *Selections from the Writings of the Bab*, p. 79)

10. Baha'u'llah, *Gleanings from the Writings of Baha'u'llah*, p. 154

11. Baha'u'llah, *Seven Valleys*, p. 21

12. 'Abdu'l-Bahá, *The Promulgation of Universal Peace*, p. 148.

13. Baha'u'llah, *Hidden Words*, Persian version, no. 27

14. Baha'u'llah, *The Kitab-i-Aqdas*, p. 47

15. Bahá'u'lláh, *Bahá'í Scriptures*, p. 164

Acknowledgement

The seed of this book was planted the first devotional/deepening took place at our home. At that meeting Gaye Gopaul, Sanjiv Gopaul and Mandana Sabet were present and I am grateful for their encouragement. In subsequently sessions that followed, many from the Bahá'í community of Newmarket came to support this initiative.

When the project moved to the next level of publishing the content of *7 Ways to obtain divine gifts and powers,* as blogs the editing help from Michael O'Toole, Jr. was invaluable. Also I thank thousands of readers from all continents and remotes like Mauritius and Quam who visited the blog site and gave many feedback.

Also I am grateful to Dale Lehman who edited the manuscript of this book and gave excellent suggestions as how to improved reader's experience.

About the Author

As a software and database specialist, Gopaul wrote seven books for IT professionals. He then turned his attention to writing two books on spirituality, which paved the way for a hidden passion to emerge. When crafting and completing *Tainted Justice*, a novel, a lifelong dream of Gopaul has now become reality.

Gopaul, married and father of two children, lives in Newmarket, Ontario, Canada.

More information about books by V. M. Gopaul can be found at www.vmgopaul.com. Some of them are:

Teach the Bahá'í Faith with Ease

Family Virtues: Give Your Child the Spiritual Edge

FastPencil
http://www.fastpencil.com